FIRST GENERATION TO OWN THIS BOOK

The
BEEKMAN
1802
HEIRLOOM
COOKBOOK

THE BEEKMAN
⊷ 1802 ⊶
HEIRLOOM COOKBOOK

BRENT RIDGE AND JOSH KILMER-PURCELL

WITH SANDY GLUCK

FOOD PHOTOGRAPHY BY PAULETTE TAVORMINA

STERLING EPICURE
New York

STERLING EPICURE
New York

An Imprint of Sterling Publishing
387 Park Avenue South
New York, NY 10016

© 2011 by Brent Ridge, Josh Kilmer-Purcell, and Sandy Gluck
Food Photography by Paulette Tavormina
Food Styling by Paul Grimes

Photograph of Brent Ridge and Josh Kilmer-Purcell on pages xiv-xv © 2010 by Ben Hoffmann
Designed by Alissa Faden

ISBN 978-1-4027-8709-6 (hardcover)

Library of Congress Cataloging-in-Publication Data

Ridge, Brent.
  The Beekman 1802 heirloom cookbook / Brent Ridge and Josh Kilmer-Purcell with Sandy Gluck.
     p. cm.
  Includes index.
  ISBN 978-1-4027-8709-6 (hardcover : alk. paper) 1. Cooking, American. 2. Farm life--New York (State)--
Upstate New York. 3. Farm produce--New York (State)--Upstate New York. 4. Beekman 1802 Farm (N.Y.) 5.
Cookbooks. I. Kilmer-Purcell, Josh, 1969- II. Gluck, Sandra. III. Title.
  TX715.R574 2011
  641.59747′1--dc22

                                        2010053875

Distributed in Canada by Sterling Publishing
c/o Canadian Manda Group, 165 Dufferin Street
Toronto, Ontario, Canada M6K 3H6
Distributed in the United Kingdom by GMC Distribution Services
Castle Place, 166 High Street, Lewes, East Sussex, England BN7 1XU
Distributed in Australia by Capricorn Link (Australia) Pty. Ltd.
P.O. Box 704, Windsor, NSW 2756, Australia

For information about custom editions, special sales, and premium and corporate purchases,
please contact Sterling Special Sales at 800-805-5489 or specialsales@sterlingpublishing.com.

Manufactured in China

2 4 6 8 10 9 7 5 3 1

www.sterlingpublishing.com

for generations

Acknowledgments

A book about heirlooms could easily necessitate a companion book with all the people who deserve a "thank you." To all the generations of our family who have contributed to these recipes to get them to where they are at the moment, to all the friends who've sat at the table at Beekman Farm and never hesitated to provide commentary on the shared meal, and to the millions of readers of *Beekman1802.com* who have joined our "experiment in seasonal living" and continue to inspire, we'll always invite you back for a second-helping.

Special thanks to Thom Driver, who was the first intern at Beekman Farm to experience a "Radical Sabbatical" and helped us capture the essence of Beekman 1802 in every photograph. To Angela Rae Berg who has "good taste" in all things epicurean. To all the antique stores across the country who unknowingly contributed to our collection of heirloom serving pieces including Yew Tree House Antiques and also to our friends at Williams-Sonoma and Christofle who immediately understood our concept for this book and who source and create items that are also destined to be heirlooms one day.

Lastly, to the entire team at Sterling, Paulette, and Sandy for creating a book that is worthy of being passed from one generation to the next.

Dig in.

CONTENTS

When we moved to Beekman Farm, over hill, over dale, and twenty miles from the nearest grocery store, the first lesson of our newly bucolic lives was that we would need to relinquish the overly indulgent and instantly gratified existence to which we had become accustomed. There is no twenty-four-hour diner, no corner deli, and certainly no delivery in our corner of upstate New York.

Initially, this meant careful planning of menus to prevent an extra trek to the market for a forgotten ingredient. But as we became more familiar with the territory, we learned which neighboring farm could provide fresh cows milk, where to go when the maple sap started running, and the closely guarded locations of the wild leek patches.

Over time, we grew to appreciate each season on the farm, both for what the season brought to the table and, oddly, for what it did not. Absence does indeed make the heart grow fonder. The time between the first cherry blossoms and the arrival of their sour fruit, and the cold months between the last tomato and the first, now seems to reinforce that there are true cycles in life—an important fact somehow lost in a world in which everything is always available.

When we started developing recipes for our website, *Beekman1802.com*, we let the ideas flow not just from the fertile reaches of our imagination, but also from what was coming from the ground. In the spring, the desire to devour the essence of each sweet pea led us to the recipe for pea pod risotto. The long, verdant beans of summer became our green bean slaw. Autumn meant stuffed apple dumplings, and even in winter, as we were scraping the bottom of the barrel for remnants of the harvest, we managed some soul-satisfying soups, stews, and casseroles.

Continue

Each of these became Beekman heirlooms—recipes that we will make every year, recipes that we pass along to friends and family on scraps of paper. They are now as much a part of the story and life of Beekman 1802 Farm as are the house, the barn, and the land.

Why "Heirloom" Recipes?

"Heirlooms" of any type have a sentimental or intrinsic value greater than their assigned monetary figure. They are often irreplaceable, and because of this they are treasured and passed down from one generation to the next.

When we started working with our friend Sandy Gluck, the former food editor for Martha Stewart's *Everyday Food* magazine, our goal was to create recipes that reflected our food heritage as well as how we live today. We wanted them to be simple and delicious, using ingredients the minute they are plucked out of the garden—recipes for every day *and* for special occasions. We wanted them to be recipes that would be passed from one generation to the next.

Each recipe has a blank note space for your personal annotation, and many of the recipes are accompanied by suggested variations so that you can adapt them to create heirloom recipes for your own family. If you come up with a unique twist, of course we want to know about it, so we've created a special section on *Beekman1802.com* where you can share your recipe *and* read how others have made the recipe their own, too.

We've also included photographs of vegetables from the Beekman 1802 heirloom vegetable garden throughout the book, styled to look like Dutch master still-life paintings. Most important, we've included several pages (see overleaf) for you to transcribe your own family's heirloom recipes either for safekeeping or for presentation of this book as a gift. Practice your handwriting!

Whether it is in the preparation or the presentation, the food we eat, where it comes from, and how it is consumed contribute to the narrative of our lives. We hope that each of these recipes becomes a part of your own story.

PORKY

AT BEEKMAN 1802, WE CELEBRATE THE SEASONS BY
GATHERING FAMILY AND FRIENDS AROUND OUR TABLE.

Like all of the products inspired by our life on the farm,
this heirloom cookbook was designed to be worthy of
passing along to the next generation. As you adapt each
of these recipes for the particular tastes of your own
family, please visit us at *Beekman1802.com*, find the
entry for the particular recipe and tell us what you did
to make it your own. This way, each recipe in this book
becomes a thousand different recipes.

We've also created this special section for you to include
your family's own heirloom recipes on the blank recipe
cards provided. You can print off additional recipe card
templates at *Beekman1802.com*.

Our hope is that you will make *our* cookbook *your*
cookbook, and it will become a keepsake for generations
to come.

POLKASPOT

BIG RED

THE FIRST TIME I REMEMBER COOKING, I WAS STARING
THROUGH A PLASTIC WINDOW WAITING PATIENTLY FOR
A FORTY-WATT LIGHTBULB TO BAKE A COOKIE IN MY
SISTER'S EASY-BAKE OVEN. The cookie didn't exactly
turn golden brown and was kind of undercooked in
the center (this probably explains why to this day I'm
much more fond of cookie dough than I am of the final
product), but nonetheless it was a *huge* step up from the
"French fries" and "spaghetti" I had been making out of
Play-Doh.

I advanced to Jell-O gelatin—mesmerized by its jewel-
tone transparency—and then to instant pudding which
my sister and I "mixed" by taking turns shaking it in an
old mayonnaise jar. Later, I would even find immense
pleasure in expertly preparing a box of Hamburger
Helper in all of its salty, fatty deliciousness.

While there's a whimsical sense of nostalgia associated
with these formative experiences, there's very little
emotional connection. Eating a Manwich or a bowl
of Campbell's soup does not bring forth the rush of
memories in the same way that sitting down to a plate
of Mom's meat loaf does.

When I was seven years old, my grandmother would
have me practice my penmanship for hours (the
doctor's handwriting I ended up with suggests that it
didn't work) as I carefully transcribed her recipes into
a wire-bound notebook. Looking at these notebooks
now brings back a wealth of memories—not just about
rainy summer afternoons spent at Mamaw's house but
also about the foods themselves and the occasions on
which they were served. Memorial Day always meant
butterscotch pie, and Thanksgiving would not be
complete without succotash made from lima beans and
white corn.

The recipes that I remember most tend to be the
simplest ones (perhaps my juvenile attention span ran
out after ten ingredients or so). Fragments of these
rainy-day writing exercises can still be seen in the way we
cook on the farm today.

BRENT

JOSH

I WAS FORTUNATE TO GROW UP IN A FAMILY WITH
SOME PRETTY GOOD COOKS. I'll start with my mother.
(Don't we all?) She was a homemaker in the 1970s with
very little money and two growing boys. Whenever
I'm trying a new recipe that seems too complicated
for its own good, I'll often check the recipe file Mom
transcribed for me when I got my first apartment.
Nearly any three-star meal at our house can find its
roots in one of my mother's recipes. The shortest line
between the kitchen and two hungry boys is often the
simplest one. And the simplest one is generally the
most elegant.

My uncle Jim Tiberia was the only Italian in a family
tree of northern Europeans. Of all the meals that I've
enjoyed over the years at a relative's house, I have to
admit, his are the ones I remember most clearly. At
most of my relatives' homes, dinner came out the
kitchen door and the emptied plates went back in. At
Uncle Jim and Aunt Mimi's home, the children worked
right beside Jim in the kitchen—tasting, adding spices,
and plating. Cooking, I learned, is a process—and a
fun one.

My uncle Arthur and his partner, Bob, lived in France.
When I finally got the chance to visit them during
college, every day began with a walk to the open-air
village market to discover what new ingredients had
come into season. The excitement over new arrivals
rivaled the buzz coming from the fashion runways
of Paris. From Bob and Arthur I learned that much
of the excitement of cooking comes from seasonal
spontaneity.

The elegance of simplicity, the joy of process, and
seasonal spontaneity. That's my food heritage. And I
can't think of a more valuable inheritance.

Every spring
is the only spring
—a perpetual
astonishment.
—ELLIS PETERS

SPRING

ur first spring on the farm—and every one since—has been one of discovery. Having spent the tail end of winter huddled by the kitchen fire, we marvel as the melting snow reveals one treasure after another.

In the barn, the first bleats of the baby goats mean that fresh milk is once again on its way. A new brood of chicks arrives by special delivery to the local post office. The first sprouts appear in the heirloom vegetable garden, and we pull on our rubber boots and take the first walk through the fields in months.

Milkweed shoots, dandelion leaves, and ramps are piled into the hod and serve as inspiring ingredients for the first impromptu meals of the season. The vibrant bursts of green are nuclear on the tongue.

Continue

DEVILED EGGS

with Smoked Trout

EVERY FAMILY SEEMS TO HAVE ONE PERSON WHOSE SOLE RESPONSIBILITY AT FAMILY GATHERINGS IS TO BRING THE DEVILED EGGS—AND THERE ARE AN ENDLESS NUMBER OF VARIATIONS. *In our version, the mayo and half-and-half make the egg yolks supercreamy, while the seasonings—curry powder, mustard, and lemon juice—work with the smoked trout to make these morsels every bit as special as the occasion.*

8 large eggs

⅓ cup half-and-half

2 tablespoons mayonnaise

1 teaspoon Dijon mustard

½ teaspoon medium-hot curry powder

½ teaspoon salt

4 ounces smoked trout, torn into small bits

2 tablespoons plus 1 teaspoon fresh lemon juice

¼ cup minced scallions

Place the eggs in a medium saucepan with cold water to cover by several inches. Bring to a boil. Remove from the heat, cover the pot, and let the eggs stand for 12 minutes. Transfer to a bowl of ice water.

Peel the eggs. Halve them crosswise and carefully scoop the yolks out into a bowl. Slice a tiny bit of egg white from the rounded sides of the egg white halves so they can stand upright. Place the egg whites on a platter and reserve. Add the half-and-half, mayonnaise, mustard, curry powder, and salt to the yolks, and mash to combine. Fold in the smoked trout. Add the lemon juice and scallions.

Spoon the mixture into the egg whites.

VARIATION If you happen to have any left over deviled eggs (hard to believe), just turn them into an egg salad. Scoop the yolk mixture into a bowl. Chop the egg whites and add them to the yolk mixture along with a little bit of chopped olives and chopped almonds. Serve on a bed of greens.

ROASTED GARLIC YOGURT CHEESE CROSTINI

EVERYONE SHOULD HAVE A FEW SIGNATURE, TASTY BITES THEY CAN WHIP UP WITH ON-HAND INGREDIENTS WHEN GUESTS ARE EXPECTED. *On the farm, we always have garlic bulbs hanging in the root cellar and an endless supply of goat milk. If you have some homemade goat milk cheese on hand, it's easy to whip up a quick bite to share with unexpected guests. In our simple crostini, roasting mellows garlic's sharp bite but retains its nutty flavor. It pairs beautifully with the mildly tangy and slightly gamey flavor of a fresh cheese made from goat milk yogurt. The cheese is spiked with lemon zest and black pepper.*

1 container (6 ounces) goat milk yogurt

1 bulb garlic (about 2 ounces)

2 teaspoons plus 2 tablespoons extra-virgin olive oil

24 thin slices of baguette (from half a baguette)

½ teaspoon grated lemon zest

¼ teaspoon salt

Freshly ground black pepper

Line a fine-mesh sieve with cheesecloth or a paper towel (or use a paper coffee filter). Spoon in the yogurt, place the sieve over a bowl to catch the whey, refrigerate, and let drain for at least 8 hours. (The longer the yogurt drains, the firmer the cheese will be.)

Preheat the oven to 350°F.

With a paring knife or scissors, remove the very top (not the root end) of the garlic bulb, cutting about ½ inch down. Place the garlic bulb in the center of a small sheet of foil. Drizzle the cut top of the garlic bulb with 1 teaspoon of the oil and enclose the garlic in the foil. Bake for 45 minutes, or until the garlic packet yields to gentle pressure.

While the garlic bakes, place the baguette slices on a large baking sheet and brush with 2 tablespoons of the oil. Bake the baguette slices alongside the garlic for 5 to 7 minutes, or until the bread is golden brown. Cool on a rack.

Remove the garlic packet from the oven and let the garlic cool in the packet. When it's cool enough to handle, squeeze the roasted garlic into a small bowl.

Add the remaining 1 teaspoon oil, and mash.

Transfer the yogurt (which should now be quite firm) to a medium bowl. Fold in the roasted garlic, lemon zest, salt, and pepper to taste.

To serve, spread about 1½ teaspoons of the yogurt cheese over each slice of baguette.

Yogurt and Yogurt Cheese

When Farmer John moved into the Beekman with his herd of goats, we were initially drowning in dairy. We tried to come up with every possible use for milk. Like most people, we initially assumed that making yogurt was a mysterious and complicated process that shouldn't be undertaken by mere mortals. As it turns out, it's quite simple—and homemade yogurt is much healthier than store-bought.

The basic process involves only three steps:

1. Heat the milk to a temperature where (good) bacteria will thrive—110 to 115°F (definitely no warmer than 120°F and no cooler than 90°F).

2. Add the starter cultures. The starter can be a few tablespoons of yogurt purchased from the grocery store. Just be sure that the ingredient list includes live bacterial cultures. They have strange names like bulgaricus, acidophilus, and thermophilus.

3. Once the starter culture is incorporated, the mixture must rest in a warm environment for anywhere from 6 to 10 hours. We put ours in the oven with nothing on but the pilot light. A heating pad on low wrapped around the container will work as well. Or set the container on top of a (not-too-hot) radiator.

After incubating, the yogurt should be chilled, and it will thicken a little further.

Note: Although homemade yogurt can be made with either pasteurized or unpasteurized milk, pregnant women, children, and those with compromised immune systems should never consume unpasteurized milk or products made from it. However, you can easily pasteurize raw milk by slowly heating it to a temperature of 140°F and holding it at that temperature for 30 minutes. (Always use stainless-steel utensils and glass containers when making yogurt to avoid contamination.) If you're pasteurizing your own raw milk for making yogurt, you can do that first and then let the milk cool down to the right temperature before adding the starter culture.

DANDELION SALAD

with Slab Bacon, Croutons, and Hot Bacon Dressing

Notes

THE SLIGHTLY BITTER, PEPPERY FLAVOR OF DANDELION GREENS FORAGED FROM THE BACKYARD IS PERFECTLY MATCHED WITH THE SALTY, SWEET, AND TANGY HOT BACON DRESSING. *Garlicky croutons add a great pungent crunch.*

4 slices (½ inch thick) whole-grain bread

2 garlic cloves, halved

2 teaspoons plus 2 tablespoons extra-virgin olive oil

6 ounces slab bacon cut into 1-inch-wide strips

2 bunches (4 ounces each) dandelion greens, torn into bite-size pieces

¼ cup red wine vinegar

1 tablespoon sugar

1½ teaspoons brown mustard

½ teaspoon salt

Preheat the oven to 350°F. Rub both sides of the bread with the cut sides of the garlic. Discard garlic. Brush the bread with 2 teaspoons oil and cut into 1-inch cubes. Spread on a baking sheet and bake for 5 to 7 minutes, or until crisp.

In a large skillet, heat the remaining 2 tablespoons of oil over medium-low heat. Add the bacon and cook until it's crisp and has rendered its fat, 7 to 10 minutes. With a slotted spoon, transfer the bacon to paper towels to drain. Reserve the skillet with the bacon fat.

Place the greens in a large salad bowl and top with the croutons. Crumble on the bacon.

Add the vinegar, sugar, mustard, and salt to the skillet with the bacon fat and bring to a boil. Pour the vinegar mixture over the dandelion greens and toss well. Serve while the dressing is still hot.

Salad Greens

Ah the varieties! We grow Red Veronica radicchio for the slightly bitter flavor and super crunch it brings to a salad; Paris White Cos romaine because it's sweet and sturdy; iceberg for Brent's cheese sandwiches; White Boston because it's tender; and Black Seeded Simpson for its reliable growing power and loose leaves.

ROASTED ASPARAGUS
with Fried Eggs and Balsamic Drizzle

SOME PEOPLE PREFER THIN ASPARAGUS, SOMETIMES CALLED PENCIL GRASS, BUT WE LIKE THE FAT SPEARS, WHICH ARE SWEETER AND TASTIER. *(If you use the thinner variety, just shorten the cooking time.) Asparagus takes well to roasting and grilling, and both methods accentuate its nutty flavor. To peel or not to peel? That's up to you. Just be sure to trim off the very bottom of the stem, as it can be tough and woody.*

12 fat asparagus spears, tough ends trimmed

3 tablespoons extra-virgin olive oil

1 teaspoon salt

⅔ cup balsamic vinegar

¼ cup orange juice

1 tablespoon honey

¼ teaspoon dried tarragon

¼ teaspoon freshly ground black pepper

Pinch of grated nutmeg

4 large eggs

Preheat the oven to 400°F.

Place the asparagus on a rimmed baking sheet or in a roasting pan, drizzle with 2 tablespoons of the oil, and toss to coat. Sprinkle with ¼ teaspoon of the salt and bake for 20 minutes, shaking the pan and turning the asparagus over, until golden brown and tender enough to be pierced with a knife. (Timing will vary depending upon the thickness and age of the asparagus.)

Meanwhile, in a medium skillet, combine the vinegar, orange juice, honey, and tarragon and bring to a boil. Boil until reduced to a glaze, about 5 minutes. Add the pepper, nutmeg, and ¼ teaspoon of the salt. Set aside.

Five minutes before the asparagus is done, heat the remaining 1 tablespoon oil in a large skillet over medium heat. One at a time, crack an egg into a custard cup or small bowl and slide it into the skillet. Sprinkle the eggs with the remaining ½ teaspoon salt, cover, and cook until the egg whites are set and the yolks are still slightly runny, 3 to 5 minutes.

Divide the asparagus among 4 plates and top with an egg. Drizzle with the balsamic glaze, and serve hot.

Notes

ASPARAGUS TORTE

"USE THEM BEFORE YOU LOSE THEM" IS A FITTING MOTTO FOR THESE SENTINELS OF SPRING. *Steaming asparagus and then tossing them briefly with shallots and butter intensifies their flavor, making them sweet and buttery. Cracker meal takes the place of flour and makes the final dish just slightly custardy. Don't be tempted to use only the tips, as the stalks are very flavorful. While we haven't peeled the asparagus, feel free to do so if you like.*

2 pounds asparagus, tough ends trimmed, cut into 2-inch lengths

4 tablespoons (½ stick) unsalted butter

3 large shallots, minced

3 green garlic stalks or scallions, thinly sliced

1 teaspoon salt

10 large eggs

½ cup heavy cream

¼ cup chopped fresh basil leaves

2 tablespoons minced fresh tarragon leaves

Pinch of cayenne pepper

1¼ cups (6 ounces) shredded Blaak cheese (page 130) or other semihard cheese

½ cup cracker meal or crushed water crackers

Preheat the oven to 350°F. Grease a shallow 6-cup glass or ceramic baking dish.

Place the asparagus in a steamer basket set over (not in) 1 inch of water in a skillet or saucepan. Bring the water to a boil, cover, and steam until the asparagus are crisp-tender, about 3 minutes. Remove the steamer basket from the pan.

In a large skillet, melt the butter over medium heat. Add the shallots and garlic stalks and cook, stirring frequently, until the shallots are tender, about 3 minutes. Add the asparagus, sprinkle with ½ teaspoon of the salt, and cook for 2 minutes.

In a large bowl, whisk together the eggs, cream, basil, tarragon, cayenne, and the remaining ½ teaspoon salt. Whisk in 1¼ cups of the cheese and the cracker meal. Fold in the asparagus mixture. Transfer to the casserole, sprinkle with the remaining ¼ cup cheese, and bake for 25 to 30 minutes, or until the top is lightly browned and the center is just set.

Notes

MINT-LEMON COOLER

THERE ARE MANY VARIETIES OF MINT, SOME MORE POWERFUL THAN OTHERS. *Common mint is what you generally find in the market, but if you're shopping at a farmers' market, you may find spearmint (pretty powerful), lemon mint, and a host of others. We have at least four varieties growing right outside the kitchen door, so we can easily grab handfuls every time we come in from the barn or garden. Even the scent is instantly refreshing. Crushing the mint (called muddling) with the sugar helps to release the flavorful oils in the leaves.*

MINT SYRUP
½ cup sugar

1 cup packed torn fresh mint leaves

1 cup water

⅛ teaspoon salt

MINT-LEMON COOLER (FOR 1 DRINK)
¼ cup mint syrup

3 tablespoons fresh lemon juice

½ cup sparkling water

FOR THE MINT SYRUP In a small saucepan, combine the sugar and mint, and using a wooden spoon, crush the leaves with the sugar. Add the water and salt and bring to a boil. Boil for 1 minute, stirring until the sugar has dissolved. Remove from the heat, cover, and let steep until the syrup reaches room temperature. Strain and refrigerate until ready to use.

FOR THE COOLER In a tumbler, combine the syrup, lemon juice, and sparkling water. Serve immediately.

VARIATION Add a little bourbon to your Mint-Lemon Cooler and this could easily become your Kentucky Derby day drink.

PASTA
with Asparagus, Peas, Ham, and Almonds

SOMETIMES EVEN HEIRLOOM RECIPES CAN BENEFIT FROM A LITTLE POLISHING. *This classic pasta dish is enlivened by the addition of fresh tarragon, which gives it a slightly lemony-anise flavor. Instead of Parmesan, we usually use the aged goat milk cheese that we make at the farm.*

8 ounces linguine

2 teaspoons extra-virgin olive oil

1 pound asparagus, tough ends trimmed, cut into 2-inch lengths

1 cup half-and-half

½ pound Virginia or Black Forest ham, in one thick piece, cut into cubes

1 cup fresh or frozen (no need to thaw) peas

1 tablespoon chopped fresh tarragon

1 teaspoon salt

½ teaspoon freshly ground black pepper

¾ cup grated Parmesan cheese

⅓ cup slivered almonds, toasted (see below)

In a large pot of boiling salted water, cook the linguine according to package directions. Drain and return the pasta to the pot.

Meanwhile, in a large skillet, heat the oil over medium heat. Add the asparagus and cook until bright green, about 2 minutes. Add the half-and-half and bring to a boil. Add the ham, peas, tarragon, salt, and pepper and cook until the peas are crisp-tender, about 3 minutes.

Remove from the heat and add to the pasta. Add the Parmesan and almonds and toss to combine.

Toasting Nuts

Place nuts in a baking pan or on a rimmed baking sheet (so they won't roll off) and bake at 350°F until fragrant and crisp, shaking the pan once or twice, 7 to 10 minutes. If you have only a small amount of nuts to toast and don't want to turn on the oven, place them in a small ungreased skillet and cook them over medium-low heat, tossing frequently, until crisp and fragrant. They will toast very quickly, so be vigilant

Notes

SPINACH SALAD
with Nasturtiums, Grapes, and Goat Feta Cheese

IN THIS SALAD, SOFT SPINACH LEAVES ARE COMPLEMENTED BY THE PEPPERY BITE OF NASTURTIUM. *You can often find packages of nasturtium flowers in a riot of colors at farmers' markets, or if you're lucky, a generous friend will share what he or she is growing. Grapes add just a touch of sweetness here, and the chives, oniony and crisp, add yet another dimension. If you can't find a goat feta, use another type of feta or your favorite soft goat cheese.*

2 tablespoons extra-virgin olive oil

1 tablespoon balsamic vinegar

2 teaspoons honey

½ teaspoon salt

8 ounces (8 cups packed) spinach leaves, preferably flat-leaf or baby

2 cups loosely packed edible (not sprayed) nasturtium flowers and leaves

1 cup seedless red grapes, halved lengthwise

3 flowering chives, greens thinly sliced, flowers torn

4 ounces goat feta, crumbled

In a large bowl, whisk together the oil, vinegar, honey, and salt until well combined. Add the spinach, nasturtium flowers and leaves (tear leaves if large), grapes, and chives, and toss to coat.

Divide the salad among 4 serving plates and scatter the cheese over the top.

Spinach

Whether we're talking curly or flat-leaf, or a blended variety, or even baby spinach, the flavor is pretty much the same. The big difference has to do with how dirty they might be. Curly varieties hold on to their grit, while the flat-leaf variety is easier to clean.

That said, here's how to clean them all: Place the spinach (leaves and most of the stem) in a bowl of cool water and slosh it around. Let it sit for a bit for the grit to settle on the bottom of the bowl; then scoop out the leaves with your hands, taking care not to agitate the water. Repeat until no grit remains.

Notes

PEA POD RISOTTO

IF YOU'VE EVER SPENT ANY TIME ON OUR WEBSITE (*Beekman1802.com*), YOU'LL KNOW THAT WE CAN BE RATHER RHAPSODIC ABOUT THE ARRIVAL OF THE SPRING PEAS. *This risotto ensures that you'll wring every last drop of sweetness out of them.*

3 pounds fresh pea pods	Salt
8 cups Chicken Stock (recipe follows) or reduced-sodium canned broth	Freshly ground black pepper
3 carrots with tops (leave tops on one), halved lengthwise	4 slices pancetta or bacon
	1 small bunch scallions, chopped
1 medium onion, halved	1 cup dry white wine
3 sprigs flat-leaf parsley	1¾ cups Arborio rice
3 sprigs fresh oregano (optional)	½ cup grated Parmesan cheese
3 sprigs fresh lemon thyme (optional)	

Shell the peas (you should have about 3 cups) and reserve the pods.

Rinse the pea pods and place them in large pot with the chicken stock, carrots (with top), onion, parsley, oregano (if using), and lemon thyme (if using). Bring to a boil, reduce to a simmer, and cook for 1 hour.

Strain the broth into a large bowl. Discard the carrots, onion, and herb sprigs. Set a food mill over the bowl of broth, add the pea pods, and puree them into the broth. Return the broth to the original pot and return to a simmer. Season with salt and pepper to taste.

In a large heavy pot, cook the pancetta over medium-high heat until the fat begins to appear clear. Add the scallions and cook until just tender, about 1 minute. Add the wine and shelled peas. Stir to coat with fat, and simmer, uncovered, until the wine is mostly evaporated, about 1 minute.

Add the rice to the pot and stir over high heat until very slightly browned and a little translucent. Add one ladleful of the pod broth. Stir the rice, and when the broth is mostly absorbed, add another ladleful. Continue adding more pod broth by the ladleful, stirring well before adding another. The rice should start to form a creamy texture, but it should still be a teeny bit al dente; it should not turn into mush. (You may not need all of the broth.)

Serve hot, topped with the Parmesan.

VARIATION For a vegetarian version, make the pea broth with water instead of chicken stock. Omit the pancetta and use 2 tablespoons olive oil when you cook the scallions.

Chicken Stock

STOCK IN THE FREEZER IS LIKE MONEY IN THE BANK: READY WHEN YOU NEED IT AND USEFUL IN SO MANY WAYS. *When chicken legs or necks and backs are on sale, you can use them instead of pieces of the whole bird to create*

1 whole chicken (3½ pounds)

1 onion, unpeeled, quartered

1 large carrot, thinly sliced

1 large celery stalk, thinly sliced

1 cup leek greens (optional)

⅓ cup parsley sprigs

3 garlic cloves, unpeeled

2 tablespoons tomato paste

8 black peppercorns

a stock with even greater depth of flavor. This recipe makes about 9 cups. Remove the giblets and neck. Cut the chicken into 10 pieces (wings, thighs, drumsticks, and breasts cut into 4 pieces). In a large pot, combine the chicken, giblets (but not the liver), neck, and 12 cups water. Bring to a boil, skimming any foam that comes to the surface.

Add all the remaining ingredients and return to a boil. Reduce to a simmer, partially cover, and cook for 2½ hours. Strain and let cool to room temperature.

The stock will keep in the fridge for 3 days. For longer storage, freeze it in portion sizes that you are likely to use, or freeze it in ice cube trays and then once the cubes are frozen pop them into freezer bags. Frozen stock will keep for at least 3 months.

ROAST LEG OF LAMB
with Fresh Mint Sauce

THE RUB FOR THE LAMB HAS A DECIDEDLY MOROCCAN FEEL, WITH CUMIN, CORIANDER, AND DRIED MINT, AND THE SAUCE IS NOT THE TRADITIONAL SWEET SAUCE THAT GOES WITH LAMB. *Rather, it's a sprightly, fresh-tasting vinegar-based sauce made with fresh mint and garlic.*

LAMB

1 tablespoon coarse salt

4 teaspoons ground coriander

2 teaspoons ground cumin

2 teaspoons dried mint

2 teaspoons sugar

1 teaspoon dried oregano

½ teaspoon freshly ground black pepper

1 boneless leg of lamb, about 5½ pounds

1 tablespoon olive oil

SAUCE

5 garlic cloves, peeled

4 cups fresh mint leaves

½ cup fresh parsley leaves

¾ cup extra-virgin olive oil

¼ cup cider vinegar

2 teaspoons Dijon mustard

2 teaspoons sugar

1 teaspoon table salt

¾ teaspoon ground coriander

¾ teaspoon ground cumin

FOR THE LAMB In a small bowl, stir together all the spices. Open the lamb so that it lies flat, and season both sides with the spice mixture. Roll the lamb up, tie it into a neat bundle, and refrigerate for at least 1 hour or up to overnight.

Preheat the oven to 425°F. Place the lamb in a roasting pan and rub with the oil. Roast for 30 minutes, or until the outside has a nice crust. Reduce the oven temperature to 300°F and roast for 40 to 45 minutes, or until an instant-read thermometer inserted in the center of the roast registers 145°F for medium rare. Remove from the oven, tent with foil, and let stand for 20 minutes before slicing and serving with the sauce.

FOR THE SAUCE In a small pot of boiling water, cook the garlic for 45 seconds. Add the mint and cook for 15 seconds. Drain and squeeze the mint dry. Transfer the mint and garlic to a blender, add the remaining ingredients, and blend until smooth. Add 2 tablespoons water and blend until well combined.

LAMB BURGERS
with Cucumber-Yogurt Sauce

CORIANDER, CUMIN, AND OREGANO ARE OFTEN USED TO SEASON LAMB AS THEY IDEALLY COMPLEMENT ITS RICHNESS. *Coriander has a slight citrus flavor, cumin has a warm, nutty taste, and oregano is herbal. Ground lamb, generally from the shoulder, is quite fatty, and that's why there's no fat added to the pan when sautéing these burgers.*

2½ teaspoons ground coriander

1½ teaspoons ground cumin

1½ teaspoons dried oregano

¾ teaspoon salt

1½ pounds ground lamb

1 container (6 ounces) Greek yogurt

2 teaspoons olive oil

1 teaspoon fresh lemon juice

2 small Kirby cucumbers, peeled in stripes, halved lengthwise and thinly sliced crosswise

¼ cup chopped fresh dill

2 tablespoons chopped fresh cilantro (leaves and stems)

In a small, dry skillet combine the coriander and cumin and heat over low until the spices are lightly toasted and fragrant, about 1 minute. Transfer to a bowl and add the oregano, ½ teaspoon of the salt, and the lamb, and mix to combine. Shape into 4 patties about 1 inch thick.

In a small bowl, whisk together the yogurt, oil, lemon juice, and remaining ¼ teaspoon salt. Add the cucumbers, dill, and cilantro, and mix to combine. Refrigerate until ready to use.

Heat a large cast-iron or nonstick skillet over medium heat (no need to add oil, as the lamb has enough fat). Add the patties and cook for 3 to 5 minutes per side for medium rare. Serve the lamb burgers with the cucumber-yogurt sauce.

CURRANT-GLAZED BAKED HAM

EASTER DINNER ALWAYS MEANT A HAM ON THE TABLE. *Pineapple juice spiked with cinnamon, cloves, and bay leaves keeps the ham moist as it cooks while also imparting a mildly sweet flavor. Red currant jelly combined with mustard and brown sugar makes a sweet and tangy glistening glaze.*

1 fully cooked, bone-in half ham (6 to 8 pounds), preferably from the butt end

1 cup pineapple juice

1 cinnamon stick, split

8 whole cloves

2 bay leaves

1/2 cup red currant jelly

2 tablespoons brown mustard

2 tablespoons light brown sugar

1 1/2 teaspoons ground ginger

Preheat the oven to 325°F.

Place the ham on a rack in a roasting pan with a lid. Using a sharp knife, score the fat on top of the ham in a diamond pattern. Pour the pineapple juice and 1/2 cup water into the bottom of the pan along with the cinnamon stick, cloves, and bay leaves. Cover the ham (if you don't have a covered roasting pan, oil a large piece of foil and cover the pan, oiled side down); roast for 45 minutes.

In a small skillet, melt the jelly over low heat. Stir in the mustard, brown sugar, and ginger.

Uncover the ham and brush it with one-third of the jelly mixture. Bake for 10 minutes. Brush with half the remaining jelly mixture, baste with the pan juices, and bake for 10 minutes. Brush the ham with the remaining jelly mixture and bake for 10 to 15 minutes, or until an instant-read thermometer registers 140°F.

Let the ham rest for 10 minutes before slicing.

VARIATION For a true southern taste, swap in cola for the pineapple juice. Omit the currant glaze. After the ham has baked for 45 minutes, uncover and baste with the pan juices. Bake for 10 minutes; then baste again with the pan juices. Bake for another 10 minutes; then lightly brush the ham all over with mustard. Lightly sprinkle all over with brown sugar, pressing into the mustard and there. Bake for the final 10 to 15 minutes.

Notes

HAM & CHEESE STRATA

THIS IS THE PERFECT COMPANY BREAKFAST: CUSTARDY FROM FRESH FARM EGGS, MILK, AND LOTS OF CHEESE AND—BEST OF ALL—ASSEMBLED THE NIGHT BEFORE. *Not just a convenience for the host, the strata sitting overnight makes the dish more custardy. When we know we're having a crowd for breakfast on the farm, a strata is our go-to dish.*

8 ounces Italian bread, cut into ½-inch-thick slices (about 16), lightly toasted

6 ounces smoked ham, diced

1½ cups (6 ounces) shredded sharp Cheddar cheese

8 large eggs

3 cups milk

¾ teaspoon salt

Pinch of cayenne pepper

Grease a shallow 2-quart baking dish. Arrange a layer of bread, a layer of ham, and a layer of cheese in the baking dish. Repeat, making one more layer.

In a large bowl, whisk together the eggs, milk, salt, and cayenne and pour over the bread, ham, and cheese. Cover and refrigerate for at least 3 hours and up to overnight.

Preheat the oven to 350°F.

Uncover the strata and place it on a rimmed baking sheet. Bake for 1½ hours, or until the strata is puffed, golden brown, and set. Let the strata stand for 10 minutes before serving.

VARIATIONS

- Substitute 2 cups of cooked vegetables (such as asparagus, broccoli, or chopped spinach) for the ham.
- Make a chicken sausage and apple strata by dicing a large sweet apple and sautéing it in 2 teaspoons of butter until crisp-tender. Use 6 ounces of smoked chicken sausage, thinly sliced, instead of ham. Layer the apple along with the sausage.
- Swap in 6 ounces of sliced Canadian bacon for the ham and use Gruyère or Swiss cheese in place of the Cheddar.

Notes

CHICKEN BREASTS
with Spinach and Farmers' Cheese

FARMERS' CHEESE IS SIMILAR IN FLAVOR TO COTTAGE CHEESE OR RICOTTA, BUT IT HAS A MUCH DRIER TEXTURE. *Its mildness pairs well with the stronger flavors of fresh oregano in the stuffing for these lemon-baked chicken breasts.*

Notes

1 tablespoon unsalted butter

¼ cup minced shallots

8 ounces spinach, tough stem ends trimmed

½ teaspoon sugar

¾ teaspoon salt

1 package (7.5 ounces) farmers' cheese

2 large eggs

2 teaspoons extra-virgin olive oil

1 teaspoon chopped fresh oregano

½ teaspoon freshly ground black pepper

4 bone-in, skin-on chicken breast halves

2 tablespoons fresh lemon juice

Preheat the oven to 400°F.

In a large skillet, heat the butter over medium-low heat. Add the shallots and cook until tender, about 5 minutes. Add the spinach by handfuls, adding more to the pan after each batch wilts. Sprinkle with the sugar and ¼ teaspoon of the salt, and cook until the liquid has evaporated, about 8 minutes.

Transfer the spinach mixture to a medium bowl. Stir in the farmers' cheese, eggs, oil, oregano, pepper, and remaining ½ teaspoon salt.

Carefully slip your fingers underneath the skin of the chicken, loosening it but not removing it. Pack the spinach mixture under the skin.

Place the chicken on a rimmed baking sheet and sprinkle the lemon juice over the top. Bake for 30 to 35 minutes, or until the filling is set and the chicken is cooked through.

VARIATION Use the same filling to stuff pasta shells or manicotti. You can also switch up the herbs, replacing the oregano with marjoram or basil.

LINGUINE
with Peas and Garlic Scapes

THE GENTLE HINT OF GARLIC FROM SCAPES IS A GREAT ADDITION TO THE CLASSIC COMBINATION OF MINT AND PEAS, AND JUST A TOUCH OF FRESH LAVENDER PEAKS THE FLAVOR. *Peas are definitely a labor of love (for each pound of peas in the pod, you get about 1 cup shelled), but, yes, they are worth it!*

8 ounces linguine

1 tablespoon extra-virgin olive oil

½ cup thinly sliced garlic scapes

1½ pounds fresh pea pods, shelled (1½ cups peas), or frozen peas

¼ cup chopped fresh mint leaves

1 tablespoon chopped fresh lavender (not sprayed)

Salt

3 tablespoons cold unsalted butter, cut into bits

In a large pot of boiling salted water, cook the linguine according to package directions.

Meanwhile, in a large skillet, heat the oil over medium heat. Add the garlic scapes and cook until tender, 3 to 5 minutes. Add the peas, ¼ cup water, the mint, and the lavender. Season with salt and cook until the peas are bright green and crisp-tender, 1 to 2 minutes.

Drain the pasta and return it to the pot. Add the pea mixture and the cold butter, swirling until the butter is creamy and coats the pasta. Season with salt.

Garlic Scapes

As a garlic bulb grows, it sends out a scape, a curved stem with a flower bud at the end. Usually these are cut off to allow the growing power of the plant to concentrate in the garlic bulbs; nowadays garlic scapes are showing up in farmers' markets everywhere. When young, garlic scapes are tender and taste something like a cross between garlic and scallions. They are mildly assertive but not overpowering. If you grow garlic yourself, be sure to catch the scapes early. As the plant grows, they get tough and woody.

Notes

MIXED GREENS TART

IN ONE CORNER OF THE PROPERTY, THERE'S A PATCH OF RAMPS (OTHERWISE KNOWN AS WILD LEEK), AND ONE OF OUR FAVORITE SPRINGTIME RITUALS IS A RAMP HUNT. *Though you probably don't have a similar patch of ramps nearby, you can still enjoy the flavor of leeks with the domesticated version. Leeks—which look like scallions on steroids—have a mellow onion flavor that marries well with strongly flavored greens such as escarole.*

Basic Pie Dough (recipe follows)

2 tablespoons unsalted butter

3 leeks, white and light green parts, halved lengthwise and cut crosswise into ½-inch slices, well washed (page 110)

1 small head escarole, cut into ½-inch chunks

3 garlic cloves, thinly sliced

3 large eggs

1 package (7.5 ounces) farmers' cheese

½ cup half-and-half

1 teaspoon salt

On a lightly floured work surface, roll the dough out to a 13-inch round. Fit the dough into a 10-inch tart pan with a removable bottom. Trim the excess dough and form a high border. Refrigerate for 30 minutes.

Preheat the oven to 350°F.

In a large skillet, heat the butter over medium heat. Add the leeks and cook until they begin to wilt, about 5 minutes. Add the escarole and garlic and cook, stirring occasionally, until both the leeks and escarole are tender and any liquid has evaporated, about 15 minutes. Cool slightly; then transfer to the tart shell.

Place the tart shell on a rimmed baking sheet. In a large bowl, whisk together the eggs, farmers' cheese, half-and-half, and salt. Pour the mixture over the vegetables. Bake for 45 minutes; then increase the oven temperature to 425°F and bake for 15 minutes, or until puffed and set. Serve warm, at room temperature, or chilled.

VARIATION Swap in 2 cups of cooked vegetables (any combo) for the leeks and the escarole.

BASIC PIE DOUGH

IT'S SURPRISING WHAT YOU CAN MAKE IF YOU HAVE THE RECIPE FOR
A BASIC PIE DOUGH. *After a lot of experimenting, we found that the
combination of butter and lard makes the flakiest, best-tasting pie or tart
shell. We have easy access to lard because we render it here at the farm,
but you might have trouble locating fresh lard (and it must be fresh). If you
can't find lard—or prefer not to use it—simply make this with a total of
8 tablespoons of butter. It'll still be perfect. (P.S. The dough can be easily
doubled for a double-crust pie.)*

1¼ cups all-purpose flour, spooned and
    leveled (page 165)

1 tablespoon sugar

¼ teaspoon salt

4 tablespoons cold unsalted butter, cut
    into bits

4 tablespoons cold lard, cut into bits

3 to 4 tablespoons ice water

In a large bowl, whisk together the flour, sugar, and salt. With a pastry blender
or two knives used scissors fashion, cut in the butter and the lard until
pea-size lumps remain. Gradually add the ice water until the dough begins to
come together but doesn't clean the sides of the bowl. Add just enough of the
ice water so the mixture holds together when pinched between two fingers.

    Alternatively, in a food processor, pulse together the flour, sugar, and salt. Add
the butter and lard and pulse 10 times or until large pea-size lumps are formed.
With the motor running, gradually add the ice water until the dough begins to
come together but doesn't clean the sides of the bowl. Add just enough of the ice
water so the mixture holds together when pinched between two fingers.

    Shape into a disk, wrap in wax paper or plastic wrap, and refrigerate for at
least 1 hour, or up to 2 days. (The dough may also be well wrapped and frozen up
to 3 months.)

Notes

FRESH PEAS

Stewed with Lettuce

BECAUSE JUST-PICKED PEAS ARE SO SWEET, YOU MAY FIND THAT AS YOU SHELL THEM, YOU EAT MORE THAN END UP IN THE POT. *The lettuce in this dish gives moisture to the peas without the addition of water, and the mint and tarragon provide light licorice notes.*

1 tablespoon unsalted butter

2 scallions, thinly sliced

1½ cups shredded leaf lettuce

2 pounds fresh pea pods, shelled (2 cups peas) or frozen peas

2 tablespoons chopped fresh mint leaves

1 teaspoon chopped fresh tarragon, marjoram, or summer savory leaves

½ teaspoon sugar

½ teaspoon salt

In a medium saucepan, melt 1½ teaspoons of the butter over medium heat. Add the scallions and lettuce and cook until the lettuce has wilted, about 2 minutes.

Add the peas, mint, tarragon, sugar, and salt, and stir to combine. Cover and cook until the peas are tender, 4 to 5 minutes. Remove from the heat and swirl in the remaining 1½ teaspoons butter.

Peas

All that shelling. It is indeed a labor of love, as a pound yields about a cup of peas. But they're far sweeter than even sugar snaps. Well, at least they are when you grow them yourself. Like corn, they begin converting their starches to sugar the moment they're picked.

Sadly, they're not the most efficient of plantings. You need some sort of trellis. And they don't really yield that much per vine. And then, one warm night and they stop producing altogether. But when the stars line up and we get a decent crop, they make us happier than tomatoes do. Yes, we said they make us happier than tomatoes do.

Notes

Sorrel Mashed Potatoes

WE ALL TEND TO LOVE MOM'S MASHED POTATOES (EVEN IF THEY ARE LUMPY), BUT THAT DOESN'T MEAN THAT FROM TIME TO TIME YOU CAN'T EXPERIMENT WITH NEW FLAVOR COMBINATIONS. *In some ways, the blandness of the potato acts as a perfect palette for creativity. Sorrel, as you'll see, adds its signature tartness. You'll be amazed that one bunch of sorrel will melt down to as little as 2 tablespoons, but, boy, will it be flavorful.*

1½ pounds baking potatoes, peeled and sliced

4 tablespoons (½ stick) unsalted butter

3 bunches sorrel (about 2 ounces each), tough ends trimmed, leaves torn

¾ cup milk

¾ teaspoon salt

In a medium saucepan, combine the potatoes with salted water to cover. Bring to a boil, reduce to a simmer, and cook until the potatoes are fork tender. Drain and return them to the pan.

Meanwhile, in a medium skillet, melt 2 tablespoons of the butter over low heat. Add the sorrel and cook, stirring occasionally, until it's very tender and soft, about 4 minutes.

With a potato masher or a handheld mixer, mash the potatoes with the milk, salt, and remaining 2 tablespoons butter. Stir in the melted sorrel and serve.

Sorrel

Sorrel's flavor is similar to that of mild spinach with a lemony kick. Also called sour grass, French sorrel, sour dock, and a host of other names, the bright green leaves are pleasantly sour. A few leaves added to a salad offer a refreshing surprise. When it is cooked, sorrel gets very, very soft and tender, and it pretty much melts into whatever you are making. Jamaican sorrel, by the way, is something altogether different; the red leaves are dried, then used to make a refreshing drink.

Notes

CREAMED SPINACH

SHALLOW-STEAMING THE SPINACH HELPS IT RETAIN SOME OF ITS SWEETNESS. *This side dish has got to be up there with other comfort foods— it's mild, sweet, and creamy.*

1 pound spinach, tough stem ends trimmed, cut into ½-inch-wide ribbons and rinsed

1 tablespoon unsalted butter

2 scallions, thinly sliced

2 tablespoons all-purpose flour

1½ cups half-and-half

½ teaspoon salt

Pile the spinach, with some of its water clinging to it, into a very large skillet or a Dutch oven. The spinach will be high in the pan, but not to worry: it'll shrink considerably as it cooks. Cover the pan and cook over medium-low heat until the spinach has wilted, about 5 minutes. Drain any liquid remaining in the pan.

Meanwhile, in a medium saucepan, melt the butter over medium heat. Add the scallions and cook, stirring frequently, until tender, about 2 minutes. Sprinkle in the flour and cook for 1 minute.

Gradually whisk in the half-and-half, add the salt, and cook, whisking constantly, until lightly thickened and smooth, about 3 minutes. There will be some texture because of the scallions, but it should not have lumps of flour. Stir in the spinach and cook for 3 minutes to blend the flavors.

Notes

SAUTÉED RADISHES

RADISHES ARE SUCH A BUMPER CROP THAT WE'VE COME UP WITH MANY USES THAT GO FAR BEYOND SLICING THEM UP IN A SALAD. *In this recipe, we sauté radishes in a little butter (cooking mellows their peppery bite) and toss them with a little bit of sugar and some cider vinegar to make them both sweet and sour.*

1 tablespoon unsalted butter

12 radishes, quartered (scant 2 cups)

¼ teaspoon salt

1 tablespoon sugar

2 tablespoons cider vinegar

In a medium skillet, melt the butter over medium heat. Add the radishes and salt and cook, tossing frequently, until the cut sides of the radishes have browned, about 5 minutes.

Add the sugar and vinegar and cook, tossing, until the radishes are tender, about 2 minutes.

Radishes

Radishes are one of the first harvests of the spring and also one of the last in the fall. They come in all shapes and sizes—some of our favorites include Black Spanish, which forms a long, dark, carrot-shaped root; White Icicle, which is shaped like its name, but packs a spicy punch; and French Breakfast, a red oblong root with a pretty white tip.

Radishes should be set free from salads. The French enjoy theirs as an appetizer, smeared with butter and sprinkled with coarse salt. We sometimes grate them into stir-fries or serve them as a simple side dish, as here. And it's not just the root that's worth celebrating. The leaves can be added to spring salads, and if you leave them in the garden long enough to bolt, their seedpods are delicious in salads or even pickled.

Notes

ROASTED TOKYO TURNIPS

TOKYO TURNIPS ARE SMALL TURNIPS THAT TASTE VAGUELY LIKE HORSERADISH WITH A TOUCH OF SWEETNESS. *They are great as a raw vegetable, but they are spectacular roasted: A simple roast transforms them from crunchy and pungent to creamy and mellow with just a hint of pepper. If you've bought them in bunches with their tops attached, save those and cook them as explained in Cooking Greens (page 138).*

16 Tokyo turnips (about 2 pounds total)

2 tablespoons extra-virgin olive oil

½ teaspoon salt

¾ teaspoon sugar

Preheat the oven to 400°F.

Cut each turnip into 4 wedges. In a glass baking dish or a metal pan large enough to hold the turnips in a single layer, toss the turnip wedges with the olive oil. Sprinkle with the salt.

Roast for 30 minutes, tossing occasionally, until turnips are tender and browned in spots. Remove from oven, sprinkle with the sugar, and toss again.

VARIATION If Tokyo turnips aren't around, choose another variety such as purple topped or golden ball.

Notes

Goat Milk Yogurt
PANNA COTTA
with Strawberry Sauce

SERVES 4

TANGY, SWEET, AND SUPER-EASY TO MAKE, THIS DESSERT COMES
TOGETHER QUICKLY AND NEEDS LITTLE TIME IN THE FRIDGE TO SET UP.
*The mild tanginess of the milk and the yogurt is both offset and complemented
by the sweet taste of the berries. This has a clean, refreshing flavor. While
there's no panna (Italian for "cream") here, the yogurt is creamy and luscious.*

1 cup goat milk

1 envelope (¼ ounce) unflavored gelatin

½ cup sugar

½ teaspoon grated lemon zest

½ teaspoon grated lime zest

¼ teaspoon grated orange zest

½ teaspoon ground cinnamon

¼ teaspoon salt

2 cups goat milk yogurt

¾ teaspoon pure vanilla extract

2 tablespoons seedless raspberry jam
    or red currant jelly

18 strawberries, thinly sliced

Place ½ cup of the goat milk in a small bowl. Sprinkle the gelatin over the top of
the milk and set aside for 5 minutes to soften and swell.

In a small saucepan, bring the remaining ½ cup goat milk, the sugar, citrus
zests, cinnamon, and salt to a simmer. Stir in the gelatin mixture and stir just
until dissolved. Remove from the heat, transfer to a bowl, and let stand for
5 minutes.

Whisk in the yogurt and vanilla until smooth. Pour the mixture into six
8-ounce dessert cups. Chill for at least 2 hours or until set.

In a medium bowl, whisk the jam with 2 teaspoons water until smooth. Add
the strawberries and toss to coat.

To serve, spoon the strawberries on top.

VARIATIONS

• Swap in whole cow milk and regular whole-milk yogurt.

• Omit the strawberries and the jam. Thinly slice 3 stalks of rhubarb and toss
them with ¼ cup sugar. Let macerate for 30 minutes; then spoon the fruit and
its juices on the panna cottas.

RHUBARB SAUCE
with Black Pepper

THIS IS NOT YOUR GRANDMOTHER'S MUSH (THOUGH THAT WAS PRETTY GOOD TOO). *We know that not everyone likes rhubarb. But not everyone has given it a fair shake either. There are as many ways to prepare rhubarb as there are any fruit. So, instead of writing off rhubarb after one mouthful of gloppy pie, we're asking you to give rhubarb one more chance. Just one.*

Notes

1 cup sugar

2 cups rhubarb pieces (½ inch)

Grated zest of 1 orange

2 grinds black pepper

In a medium saucepan, combine the sugar and ½ cup water. Bring to a boil over medium heat. Stir to dissolve the sugar; watch carefully so as not to burn or boil over. Once the sugar is completely dissolved and the syrup is simmering, remove from the heat and immediately stir in the rhubarb, orange zest, and pepper.

Let cool to room temperature. If the rhubarb hasn't cooked enough in the cooling simple syrup, reheat to simmering for 1 minute at a time—no longer. Then allow to cool, and taste again. Do not overcook . . . rhubarb pieces will quickly fall apart.

VARIATION Use 3 tablespoons of Cointreau instead of grated orange zest.

Rhubarb

Technically, rhubarb is a vegetable, but it's eaten as a fruit and is known as the pie plant. (Yes, rhubarb suffers from an identity crisis.) We don't care what it's called. We simply love it. Cooked with sugar and a touch of vanilla, it's the springtime equivalent of applesauce. Tossed with strawberries and cooked in a pie, it can't be beat. (Sandy likes her rhubarb straight up, sugar and vanilla, even fresh ginger is okay, but hold the strawberries.) Maybe we're enamored with rhubarb because it's one of the first things to appear in our spring garden after a winter of root vegetables. (P.S. Don't eat the leaves; they're toxic.)

LEMON PUDDING CAKE

SERVES 6

THIS TYPE OF DESSERT IS CALLED A PUDDING CAKE BECAUSE AS IT BAKES IT SEPARATES INTO A CAKE LAYER [ON TOP] AND PUDDING ON THE BOTTOM.

Preheat the oven to 350°F. Grease an 8-inch square baking dish. Put a kettle of water on to boil.

1 tablespoon grated lemon zest (from about 2 lemons)

⅔ cup plus 1 tablespoon sugar

¼ cup all-purpose flour

1 cup milk

⅓ cup fresh lemon juice (from about 2 lemons)

¼ cup heavy cream

3 tablespoons unsalted butter, melted and cooled

3 large eggs, separated

¼ teaspoon salt

In a large bowl, combine the lemon zest and ⅔ cup of the sugar, mashing the zest into the sugar. Whisk in the flour, milk, lemon juice, cream, melted butter, and egg yolks until smooth.

In a separate bowl, beat the egg whites with the salt until foamy. Beat in the remaining 1 tablespoon sugar until soft peaks form. Stir about one-fourth of the egg whites into the flour mixture to lighten slightly, and then gently fold in the remaining egg whites. Pour into the baking dish.

Set the baking dish in a larger pan. Set the pan on a pulled-out oven rack, and pour in boiling water to come halfway up the sides of the baking dish. Bake for 40 minutes, or until the top is golden brown and set. Transfer the pan to a rack to cool. Serve warm.

VARIATION Make an orange pudding cake by swapping in ¼ cup orange juice, 2 tablespoons lemon juice, and 1 tablespoon grated orange zest for the lemon. Or use Meyer lemons in place of the regular lemons.

Notes

Strawberry-Rhubarb Crumble

EVERY HOME COOK SHOULD HAVE AN EASY AND TANTALIZING DESSERT IN HIS OR HER REPERTOIRE. *This is ours. A little bit of balsamic vinegar gives the dish a slight kick.*

·⦃FILLING⦄·

2 pounds strawberries, halved or quartered if large (5 cups)

1 pound rhubarb, cut into 1-inch lengths

2 tablespoons balsamic vinegar

1 cup granulated sugar

3 tablespoons all-purpose flour

¼ teaspoon salt

·⦃STREUSEL TOPPING⦄·

1 cup old-fashioned rolled oats

1 cup all-purpose flour

1 cup packed light brown sugar

10 tablespoons cold unsalted butter, cut into bits

Preheat the oven to 425°F.

FOR THE FILLING In a large bowl, combine the strawberries, rhubarb, and vinegar and toss to combine. Add the granulated sugar, flour, and salt and toss again. Transfer the mixture to a 9-inch square baking dish.

FOR THE STREUSEL TOPPING In a medium bowl, combine the oats, flour, and brown sugar. With your fingers, cut in the butter until the mixture forms large clumps. Scatter the topping over the fruit.

Place the baking dish on a rimmed baking sheet (to catch any drips) and bake for 35 to 40 minutes, or until the filling is bubbling and the topping is crisp.

VARIATION When rhubarb is not in season, you can swap in 1 pound of thawed and drained frozen mixed berries. Reduce the amount of granulated sugar to ½ cup.

STRAWBERRY SHORTCAKES

PICKING STRAWBERRIES IN THE SPRING GOES SOMETHING LIKE THIS. ONE FOR THE BASKET, ONE FOR THE MOUTH. *For the berries that actually make it back to the kitchen, a celebration of sorts is called for. Heavy cream and sour cream combine to make a superthick and tangy cream called crème fraîche. Start the crème fraîche a day before you plan on preparing the shortcakes. If your strawberries are really sweet, cut back on the sugar in the berries a little—but don't omit it altogether, as it helps to produce a lovely syrup.*

¾ cup heavy cream

⅓ cup sour cream

1 pound strawberries, thinly sliced

6 tablespoons sugar

1½ cups all-purpose flour, spooned and leveled (page 165)

2¼ teaspoons baking powder

½ teaspoon baking soda

½ teaspoon salt

6 tablespoons cold unsalted butter, cut into bits

½ cup buttermilk

In a small bowl, whisk together the heavy cream and sour cream. Cover and let stand at room temperature for at least 10 hours or until thick enough that a spoon can stand up in it.

In a medium bowl, toss the strawberries with 2 tablespoons of the sugar and set aside for at least 20 minutes.

Preheat the oven to 400°F. In a large bowl, whisk together the flour, 2 tablespoons of the sugar, and the baking powder, baking soda, and salt. With a pastry blender or two knives used scissors fashion, cut the butter into the flour mixture until pea-size lumps remain. Add the buttermilk and mix just until combined. Transfer to a floured work surface and pat the dough out to a 9-inch round about ¾ inch thick. With a 3-inch biscuit cutter, cut out 6 rounds, rerolling scraps as necessary. Transfer to a baking sheet and bake for 15 to 18 minutes, or until the tops are firm. Let cool to room temperature.

Split each biscuit in half horizontally. Stir the remaining 2 tablespoons sugar into the crème fraîche. Top the bottom half of each biscuit with berries and their syrup and 3 tablespoons of the crème fraîche. Top with the other biscuit half.

VARIATIONS

* Instead of making crème fraîche, simply whip heavy cream with a little sugar.
* For an even richer biscuit, swap in heavy cream for the buttermilk and omit the baking soda.

Strawberries

On the farm we grow small alpine berries, known as *fraises des bois* or berries of the woods, because they are small and sweet, just like wild berries. (By the way, if you're going to buy any organic fruit, we suggest that you spend the money on berries, because they're more prone to absorbing pesticides.)

To hull strawberries (which means removing the green leafy stem and the hard bit of berry just beneath it) we suggest using a paring knife. Insert it at a slight angle under the green stem; then turn the berry until you've made a cut all the way around. The stem can be gently pulled out of the berry. Of course, hulling isn't necessary when you're popping berries into your mouth. In fact, the green stem makes a nice little handle.

If you'd like to freeze strawberries, hull and place them on a baking sheet in a single layer. Freeze them on the sheet; then transfer them to freezer containers. They'll keep for up to 6 months.

Summer afternoon—summer afternoon; to me those have always been the two most beautiful words in the English language.

—HENRY JAMES

So many memories are associated with summer because there are so many daylight hours in which to make them: the smell of sheets dried by an arid breeze, the shocking cold of water on hot skin, and always, no matter how far away you are from civilization, always, the echo of children's laughter from somewhere in the distance.

More than once, a summer trip through the heirloom vegetable garden has led to an impromptu feast. Each just-plucked morsel has captured a last-second ray, and as you take a bite, you are, in fact, filling your mouth with the unparalleled taste of pure sunshine.

Continue

Mini Ham and Cheese Biscuits

BISCUITS WITH CHEESE IN THEM INSTEAD OF ON THEM MAKE PERFECT HORS D'OEUVRES FOR A PARTY. *Although these addicting little bites are ideal year-round, we tend to serve them throughout the summer on the porch at informal gatherings.*

2 cups all-purpose flour, spooned and leveled (page 165)

2 teaspoons baking powder

¼ teaspoon baking soda

½ teaspoon salt

5 tablespoons cold unsalted butter, cut into bits

1 cup (4 ounces) shredded sharp Cheddar cheese

¾ cup buttermilk

1 teaspoon Dijon mustard

½ cup hot pepper jelly

6 slices smoked ham (about ¼ pound), quartered

Preheat the oven to 425°F. Line a baking sheet with parchment paper. In a large bowl, whisk together the flour, baking powder, baking soda, and salt. With a pastry blender or two knives used scissors fashion, cut the butter into the flour mixture until pea-size lumps remain. Add the cheese and stir to combine. With a fork, mix in the buttermilk and mustard until combined. The mixture will not form a ball but will stick together when pinched.

Turn the dough out onto a lightly floured work surface and roll out ½ inch thick. With a 1½-inch biscuit cutter, cut out 24 rounds, rerolling scraps as necessary. Place on the lined baking sheet and bake for 17 to 20 minutes, or until golden brown and set.

Let cool on a rack. Split the biscuits in half horizontally. Top the bottom half with 1 teaspoon jelly and 1 piece of ham. Replace the top of the biscuit.

VARIATIONS

- Give the biscuits a little crunch by reducing the flour by 2 tablespoons and adding 2 tablespoons of cornmeal.
- For an even richer biscuit, swap in heavy cream for the buttermilk, increase the baking powder to 2½ teaspoons, and omit the baking soda.

Notes

CORN FRITTERS

SERVES 4

FOLDING BEATEN EGG WHITES INTO THE CORN BATTER MAKES THESE FRITTERS REALLY LIGHT. *Serve plain or with mayo mixed with a little ancho or chipotle chile powder, or with just a drizzle of maple syrup—cook's choice.*

1½ cups corn kernels, fresh (from 2 to 3 ears) or thawed frozen

2 scallions, thinly sliced

⅓ cup finely chopped dry-cured chorizo sausage

2 large eggs, separated

2 tablespoons unsalted butter, melted

½ cup all-purpose flour

1 teaspoon baking powder

2 teaspoons sugar

¾ teaspoon salt

2 tablespoons extra-virgin olive oil

In a large bowl, combine the corn, scallions, chorizo, egg yolks, and melted butter. In a separate bowl, whisk together the flour, baking powder, sugar, and salt. Fold the flour mixture into the corn mixture.

With a mixer, in a separate bowl, beat the egg whites to soft peaks. Gently fold the whites into the corn batter.

In a large skillet, heat the oil over medium heat. In batches, drop the fritters by mounded ¼ cup into the oil, about 4 at a time. Cook until golden brown and cooked through, about 2 minutes per side.

VARIATIONS

• For simpler fritters, omit the chorizo and scallions.

• For jazzier fritters, add some shredded sharp Cheddar to the corn mixture.

Cutting Corn

Cut off a small slice from the bottom (stalk end) of each shucked ear so it will stand upright; then, working in a rimmed baking sheet, cut from the top to the bottom to release all the corn kernels. To get every last bit of corn, run the dull side of the knife down the length of the cut cob to push out the bits of corn germ.

Notes

TOMATO AND GOAT CHEESE CROSTINI

A SIMPLE AND PERFECT APPETIZER WHEN TOMATOES ARE IN SEASON AND BURSTING WITH VINE-RIPENED FLAVOR. *Baguettes do come in different sizes, so figure you'll need at least 8 inches of bread. Italian bread works well too, although it's usually wider—in that case either make fewer crostini or more of the topping.*

½ baguette (about 8 inches), cut crosswise into 24 slices

5 tablespoons extra-virgin olive oil

5 garlic cloves–2 halved and 3 thinly sliced

3 large shallots, finely chopped

1½ pounds plum tomatoes, cut into ½-inch dice

¾ teaspoon salt

5 ounces soft goat cheese

Fresh mint leaves

Preheat the oven to 400°F.

Brush the baguette slices on both sides with 3 tablespoons of the oil. Rub the bread with the cut sides of the halved garlic; discard halved garlic. Place the bread on a baking sheet and bake until crisp and golden, turning once, about 4 minutes per side.

Meanwhile, in a large skillet, heat the remaining 2 tablespoons oil over medium heat. Add the sliced garlic and shallots and cook, stirring frequently, until the shallots are tender, about 5 minutes. Add the tomatoes and salt and cook until the tomatoes have softened but still hold their shape, about 5 minutes. Let the mixture cool slightly.

Spread the goat cheese on the crostini and top with the tomato mixture and mint leaves.

Notes

Chanterais Melon Salad

Notes

CHANTERAIS IS THE MELON THAT APPEARS MOST OFTEN ON THE BEEKMAN TABLE. *It's an heirloom French melon related to the cantaloupe. It's small and supersweet. Here the melon's sweetness is counterbalanced by peppery radishes, tart lemons, and sweet-tart grape tomatoes. While eating a bite of a lemon might seem a little odd, it bursts with flavor and only enhances the taste of the melon. Serve this as a refreshing appetizer or as a salsa to go with grilled chicken.*

1 Chanterais melon or ½ cantaloupe, seeded

1 lemon

2 teaspoons honey

½ teaspoon salt

½ cup grape tomatoes, quartered

2 radishes, thinly sliced crosswise, then cut into thin matchsticks

¼ cup small whole fresh mint leaves

With a small melon baller, scoop out melon balls. Following the curve of the lemon, cut off and discard the peel, including the membrane covering the segments. Working over a small bowl to catch the juice, cut in between the lemon segments to release them from the membranes. Cut the lemon segments in half. Squeeze the juice from the membranes into the bowl.

In a medium bowl, whisk together 2 teaspoons of the lemon juice, the honey, and the salt. Add the melon balls, lemon segments, tomatoes, radishes, and mint leaves and toss to combine.

HOMEMADE LEMONADE
with Lavender and Vanilla

HOT SUMMER DAYS AND LONG HOURS IN THE GARDEN CALL FOR AN EASY THIRST-QUENCHING DRINK. *Tart lemon juice with an underlying layer of smoothness from the vanilla and the slightly floral taste of the lavender make for a winning combination. Keep the sugar syrup on hand in your refrigerator, add some freshly squeezed lemon juice, pour over ice, and imagine you're sitting on the porch with us at the Beekman.*

½ cup sugar

2 teaspoons dried lavender

1 vanilla bean, split lengthwise

Pinch of salt

1¾ cups fresh lemon juice (from about 8 lemons)

In a small saucepan, combine the sugar, lavender, vanilla bean, salt, and 1 cup water. Bring to a boil, stirring until the sugar has dissolved. Remove from the heat, cover, and let stand for 30 minutes. Strain. (If you rinse and dry the vanilla bean, you can use it once more in another dish.)

Combine the sugar syrup and lemon juice and serve over ice.

Notes

CUCUMBER COOLER

THE COMBINATION OF CUCUMBER, CORIANDER, AND SUGAR MAKES A SIMPLE SYRUP THAT TASTES LIKE A CROSS BETWEEN VANILLA AND CITRUS. *It makes a great base for our refreshing summer cooler: just add sparkling water and a little lime juice. This same simple syrup can also be used in summer cocktails.*

CUCUMBER SIMPLE SYRUP

1½ cups water

¾ cup sugar

½ teaspoon coriander seeds

4 Kirby cucumbers (½ pound total), peeled, halved lengthwise, and thinly sliced crosswise

CUCUMBER COOLER (FOR 1 DRINK)

¼ cup Cucumber Syrup

¾ cup sparkling water

1 teaspoon fresh lime juice

3 to 4 thin slices skin-on Kirby cucumber, for garnish

FOR THE SYRUP In a small saucepan, bring the water, sugar, and coriander seeds to a boil over medium heat. Boil for 1 minute, stirring to dissolve the sugar.

Add the cucumbers to the pan, cover, remove from heat, and let stand at room temperature until the mixture is cool. Strain and discard the cucumbers and coriander. (Refrigerated, the syrup will keep for several weeks.)

FOR THE COOLER Pour the cucumber syrup into a tumbler and top it off with the sparkling water. Add the lime juice and stir to combine. Add the cucumber slices and serve while the sparkling water is still sparkling.

VARIATION For a superintense cucumber flavor, you can take this one step further. Leave the cucumbers unpeeled. Cut them into chunks and puree them in a food processor. Add the puree to the sugar syrup, cover, and let stand at room temperature until cool, then strain and store as directed.

MEAT LOAF BURGERS
with Blaak Cheese

Notes

_____
_____
_____
_____
_____
_____
_____
_____
_____
_____
_____
_____
_____
_____
_____
_____
_____
_____
_____
_____
_____
_____
_____
_____
_____

MEAT LOAF SANDWICHES HAVE BEEN A FAVORITE SINCE CHILDHOOD, SO WHY NOT FIRE UP THE GRILL AND MAKE BURGERS, MEAT LOAF STYLE? *They have the same great taste and can be on the table in about 15 minutes. Serve with a couple of thick slices of Fried Green Tomatoes (page 70) as a homespun twist on an American classic. As for the buns, we prefer brioche-like challah rolls, but that's up to you.*

2 teaspoons vegetable oil

1 medium onion, finely chopped

¾ pound ground beef chuck

½ pound ground veal shoulder

½ pound ground pork shoulder

½ cup panko bread crumbs

⅓ cup milk

2 tablespoons ketchup

2 tablespoons Dijon mustard

1 teaspoon salt

½ teaspoon rubbed sage

½ teaspoon dried thyme

6 ounces Blaak cheese (page 130), thinly sliced

In a medium skillet, heat the oil over medium heat. Add the onion and cook, stirring occasionally, until the onion is tender, about 7 minutes. Transfer to a large bowl and let cool to room temperature.

Add the beef, veal, pork, panko, milk, ketchup, mustard, salt, sage, and thyme. Mix to combine, and then shape into six 1-inch-thick patties.

Preheat the grill to medium heat. Oil the grill grates. Grill the burgers, covered, for 4 to 5 minutes, or until they've formed a crust on the bottom. Turn the burgers over and grill 3 to 4 minutes longer, until they've formed a crust on the second side. Top with the cheese and cook for 1 minute to melt the cheese.

VARIATION Of course the burger mixture also makes a splendid meat loaf. Add 2 large eggs to the meat and seasonings. Transfer the mixture to a 9 x 5-inch loaf pan and bake for 1 hour in a preheated 350°F oven. Brush the top of the loaf with ⅓ cup ketchup and bake for 10 minutes longer or until the meat loaf registers 150°F on an instant-read thermometer. Let stand for 10 minutes before slicing and serving.

TOMATO BREAD SALAD
with Cannellini Beans and Goat Feta Cheese

Notes

_____
_____
_____
_____
_____
_____
_____
_____
_____
_____
_____
_____
_____
_____
_____
_____
_____
_____
_____
_____
_____
_____
_____
_____
_____
_____

TOMATOES AND A FRUITY OLIVE OIL, DAMPEN CUBES OF TOASTED COUNTRY BREAD, MAKING THEM DELICIOUSLY MOIST WHILE STILL HOLDING THEIR SHAPE. *This is perfect to serve on a warm summer's day. It's even delicious served as a cold salad the next day, so make extra.*

8 ounces country bread, cut into 1-inch chunks

5 tablespoons extra-virgin olive oil

1 pound assorted heirloom tomatoes (of varying colors), cut into 1-inch chunks

¾ teaspoon salt

¼ cup pine nuts

1¾ cups cooked cannellini beans or 1 can (15 ounces) cannellini beans, rinsed

2 tablespoons red wine vinegar

⅓ cup torn fresh basil leaves

8 ounces goat feta cheese, crumbled

Preheat the oven to 400°F.

In a small bowl, toss the bread with 2 tablespoons of the oil. Transfer the bread to a baking sheet and bake for 7 to 10 minutes, or until crisp. Transfer to a bowl.

Add the tomatoes to the bowl with the bread, sprinkle with the salt, and toss to combine. Let sit for 20 minutes.

In a small ungreased skillet, toast the pine nuts over low heat, tossing frequently, until golden, about 5 minutes. Transfer the nuts to a plate so they don't keep cooking.

Add the beans, vinegar, basil, pine nuts, and remaining 3 tablespoons oil to the bowl with the bread and tomatoes and toss to combine. Add the cheese and toss gently.

VARIATION Swap in chunks of fresh mozzarella for the goat feta, chickpeas for the cannellini beans, balsamic vinegar for the red wine vinegar. Add ½ cup pitted and halved Gaeta olives.

FARFALLE
with Fresh Heirloom Tomato Sauce

WHEN YOU'VE GOT GREAT HEIRLOOM TOMATOES, FRESH OFF THE VINE AND BURSTING WITH SUMMER GOODNESS, THEY DON'T NEED MUCH ELSE. *In fact, this sauce is not even cooked, which makes it a perfect summertime dish. Choose meaty red heirlooms for this, along with some others with interesting colors, like green zebras and yellow taxi. A combo of any soft herbs would really work here.*

3 pounds assorted meaty heirloom tomatoes, cored

12 ounces farfalle pasta

½ cup extra-virgin olive oil

8 garlic cloves, thinly sliced

¼ teaspoon hot pepper flakes

½ cup chopped flat-leaf parsley

½ cup fresh basil leaves, torn

2 tablespoons chopped chives

1½ teaspoons salt

1 teaspoon grated orange zest

Set up a large bowl of ice and water.

Bring a large pot of water to a boil. Add the tomatoes, a few at a time, and cook for 10 seconds until the skins loosen. Scoop them out with a slotted spoon or spider and transfer to the ice water. (Let the pot of water stay at the boil.) Peel the tomatoes, halve them, and squeeze the juice and seeds through a fine-mesh sieve set over a large bowl. Discard the seeds. Coarsely chop the tomatoes and add them (and any juices) to the bowl.

Salt the boiling water, add the pasta to the pot, and cook according to package directions. Drain.

Meanwhile, in a small skillet, heat the oil, garlic, and hot pepper flakes over medium-low heat until the garlic is tender, about 5 minutes. Whisk the oil mixture into the tomatoes until well combined. Add the pasta, parsley, basil, chives, salt, and orange zest and and toss again. Adjust salt if necessary.

VARIATION To make this a heartier dish, add ½ pound fresh mozzarella cheese, cut into chunks; or 1 can (5 ounces) oil-packed tuna, drained, ⅓ cup pitted olives, coarsely chopped, and 1 tablespoon capers when adding the pasta.

Easy Eggplant Parmesan

EGGPLANT HAS A BAD REPUTATION FOR BEING A SPONGE THAT SOAKS UP OIL. *One way to avoid the problem is to bake eggplant instead of frying it. The baked eggplant slices come out crisp, golden brown, and not at all oily. When choosing eggplant, don't go over about 1 pound—the larger they are, the more seeds they have.*

1 eggplant (about 1 pound), peeled	½ cup all-purpose flour
Salt	3 tablespoons olive oil
1 cup panko bread crumbs	2 large tomatoes, sliced into 16 rounds
¾ cup grated Parmesan cheese	16 basil leaves
2 large eggs	8 ounces mozzarella, shredded

Preheat the oven to 400°F. Line a rimmed baking sheet with parchment paper. Cut the eggplant crosswise into 16 slices about ½ inch thick. Sprinkle the slices with salt, place them in a colander, and let them drain over a bowl for 30 minutes. Rinse the salt off and squeeze the eggplant slices dry.

In a shallow bowl or on a sheet of wax paper, combine the panko, Parmesan, and ½ teaspoon salt. In a separate bowl, whisk the eggs with 1 tablespoon of water until combined. Place the flour in a separate bowl or on a sheet of wax paper. Dip the eggplant slices first in the flour, shaking off the excess. Next dip them in the eggs, letting the excess drip off. Finally dip the eggplant slices in the panko mixture, pressing it to adhere.

Place the eggplant on the baking sheet and drizzle the oil over the tops. Bake for 20 minutes; then turn the eggplant over and bake for 10 minutes longer, or until tender, golden, and crisp. Top each slice with a tomato slice, then a basil leaf, and scatter the mozzarella over the top. Bake for 10 minutes, or until the cheese has melted.

VARIATION Skip the tomato, basil, and mozzarella and simply serve the eggplant slices with lemon wedges as a vegetable side dish.

Notes

SPAGHETTI AND MEATBALLS

THESE MEATBALLS ARE SO FLAVORFUL THAT THE ONLY SAUCE YOU'LL NEED IS THE SIMPLE TOMATO PUREE MIXTURE THAT THEY COOK IN. *As the puree and meatballs cook together, the sauce is enriched by the juices from the meatballs.*

3 tablespoons extra-virgin olive oil

2 cups finely chopped onion (about 1 large)

1½ pounds ground meat loaf mix (equal parts pork, veal, and beef)

⅔ cup grated Parmesan cheese, plus more for serving

½ cup panko bread crumbs

⅓ cup milk

2 large eggs

1½ teaspoons salt

⅓ cup all-purpose flour

1 can (28 ounces) crushed tomatoes in puree

2 tablespoons tomato paste

½ cup Chicken Stock (page 17) or reduced-sodium canned broth

12 ounces spaghetti or long fusilli

In a large skillet, heat 1 tablespoon of the oil over medium heat. Add the onion and cook, stirring frequently (and adding ¼ cup water if necessary), until tender, about 10 minutes. Let cool slightly.

In a large bowl, combine the sautéed onion, meat, Parmesan, panko, milk, eggs, and salt and mix gently to combine. Shape into 24 meatballs.

Dredge the meatballs in the flour, shaking off the excess. In a large deep skillet, heat the remaining 2 tablespoons oil over medium heat. In batches, add the meatballs and cook until browned all over, 3 to 4 minutes. Transfer to a plate.

Pour off any fat remaining in the skillet. Add the tomatoes, tomato paste, and stock and bring to a boil. Return the meatballs to the pan, cover, and simmer until tender and cooked through, about 35 minutes.

Meanwhile, bring a large pot of water to a boil. About 15 minutes before the meatballs are done, salt the pasta water, add the spaghetti, and cook according to package directions. Drain. Serve the spaghetti topped with meatballs and sauce and pass extra Parmesan at the table.

Notes

STUFFED PEPPERS
with Fresh Corn

PARMESAN CHEESE AND A BIT OF GARLIC TAKE THE MEAT LOAF MIXTURE IN AN ITALIAN DIRECTION, AS DOES THE TOMATO SAUCE. *For this recipe, thin- rather than thick-walled bell peppers are best, as they'll quickly get tender as they cook.*

2 tablespoons olive oil

1 medium onion, chopped

6 garlic cloves, finely chopped

1 can (15 ounces) crushed tomatoes

½ cup Chicken Stock (page 17) or reduced-sodium canned broth

Meat loaf Burgers mixture, uncooked (page 54)

2 cups shredded Parmesan cheese

2 cups fresh corn kernels (3 to 4 ears)

½ cup chopped fresh parsley

½ teaspoon salt

6 bell peppers (red, yellow, green, or a combination)

Preheat the oven to 400°F.

In a medium skillet, heat 1 tablespoon of the oil over medium heat. Add the onion and a third of the chopped garlic and cook, stirring frequently, until the onion is tender, about 7 minutes. Add the tomatoes and stock and cook for 5 minutes to blend the flavors.

In a small skillet, heat the remaining 1 tablespoon oil over low heat. Add the remaining garlic and cook, stirring, until the garlic is tender, about 2 minutes. Transfer to a large bowl.

Add the meat loaf mixture, 1½ cups of the Parmesan, the corn, the parsley, and the salt and gently mix to combine.

Cut off the stem end of the peppers and then halve the peppers lengthwise. Remove the ribs and seeds and slice the thinnest sliver from the skin side of each pepper half so it will sit flat.

Stuff the pepper halves with the meat mixture. Pour the tomato sauce into a 9 x 13-inch baking dish. Place the filled peppers in the sauce and bake for 30 minutes, or until cooked through. Sprinkle the peppers with the remaining ½ cup Parmesan and bake for 5 minutes to melt the cheese.

Notes

GRILLED SUMMER SQUASH PIZZA

SUMMER SQUASH ARE MELLOW AND BUTTERY IN TASTE AND COOK REALLY QUICKLY ON THE GRILL. *If you've got a grill with grates that are far apart, use a grill topper to cook the squash.*

4 medium yellow or golden summer squash (about 6 ounces each), cut crosswise on a deep diagonal into ¼-inch-thick slices

2 yellow pattypan squash, cut crosswise into ¼-inch-thick slices

¼ cup extra-virgin olive oil

3 garlic cloves, smashed and peeled

Salt

¾ pound homemade or store-bought pizza dough

6 ounces soft goat cheese

1 tablespoon red wine vinegar

¼ cup small fresh basil leaves

In a large bowl, combine the squash, oil, garlic, and salt to taste, and toss to coat the squash. Let stand for 1 hour. Remove and discard the garlic.

Preheat a grill to medium. Lightly oil the grill grates. Place the squash on the grill and cook until grill marks appear on one side, about 3 minutes. Turn the squash over and grill until tender, about 2 minutes. Return the squash to the bowl.

On a lightly floured work surface, roll the dough out to a 14-inch round. Place the dough on a nonstick (or floured) cookie sheet and slide the dough onto the grill. Cook until grill marks form on the underside, about 5 minutes. Turn the dough over and top with the goat cheese. Top with the squash. Sprinkle the squash with the vinegar and salt to taste. Cook until the cheese has melted, about 3 minutes. Scatter the basil over the top.

Yellow Squash

Somehow yellow squash doesn't have the bad rap that zucchini has, perhaps because it doesn't tend to get so unwieldy in size. We like the pattypan variety with scalloped edges because it's sweet, dense, and not so watery.

Zucchini, Pepper, and Tomato Gratin

ZUCCHINI, BELL PEPPER, TOMATOES, AND FRESH HERBS: A SUMMER GARDEN, ALL IN ONE DISH. *Tossing the panko bread crumbs with Parmesan cheese and oil helps them brown and crisp, making a nice topping for the soft, tender vegetables underneath.*

3 cloves garlic, smashed and peeled

4 tablespoons extra-virgin olive oil

1 large onion, halved and thinly sliced

1 cup panko bread crumbs

½ cup grated Parmesan cheese

1 pound zucchini, cut crosswise into ¼-inch slices

1 large red bell pepper, diced

1 pound tomatoes, halved, seeded, and coarsely chopped

1 teaspoon finely chopped fresh rosemary

1 teaspoon finely chopped fresh oregano

1 teaspoon salt

Preheat the oven to 400°F. Rub a large shallow baking dish with 1 clove of the garlic and discard the clove. Coarsely chop the remaining 2 garlic cloves.

In a large skillet, heat 2 tablespoons of the oil over medium heat. Add the chopped garlic and onion and cook, stirring frequently, until the onion is very tender, about 10 minutes.

In a medium bowl, toss together the panko, Parmesan, and remaining 2 tablespoons oil.

Arrange the vegetables in stripes across the width of the dish: Starting at one end of the baking dish, make a row of zucchini, followed by one of onions, then peppers, then tomatoes. Repeat the stripes until you've used all the vegetables (you may have to do this in layers, depending on the size of your dish).

Sprinkle the vegetables with the rosemary, oregano, and salt. Scatter the panko mixture over the top and bake for 45 minutes, or until the vegetables are tender.

Notes

HERB GREEN BEANS
with Red Onions

DURING THE SUMMER, WE (ALMOST) BECOME VEGETARIANS. *In this fresh bean dish, the lemon juice is added just before serving to keep the beans a beautiful bright green. Adding it any earlier would cause the beans to discolor.*

1 pound green beans, stem ends trimmed

¼ cup extra-virgin olive oil

1 teaspoon Dijon mustard

2 garlic cloves, smashed and peeled

½ teaspoon salt

1 small red onion, halved and thinly sliced

¼ cup chopped fresh dill, basil, or parsley (or a mix of all three)

1 teaspoon grated lemon zest

¼ cup fresh lemon juice

In a large pot of boiling salted water, cook the green beans until crisp-tender, about 3 minutes. Transfer the beans to a colander and rinse under cold water to stop the cooking.

In a large bowl, whisk together the oil, mustard, garlic, and salt. Add the onion, herbs, lemon zest, and green beans and toss to coat. Refrigerate at least 2 hours or up to overnight.

To serve, remove and discard the garlic, add the lemon juice, and toss well.

Green Beans

There are more varieties of green beans than nearly any other vegetable, but they all have one thing in common—it's best to pick them early. The younger they are, the more tender they are, and any strings are easier to remove—simply snap off the stem end and pull gently along the seam to remove the strings. If the beans are young enough, there's no need to snap off the pointed ends—they will become tender when cooked.

If you're unable to harvest and use the beans quickly enough, leave them on the vine or bush until the plants die and the pods dry. The beans inside will become hard and dry and, once shelled, can be kept and used all winter.

Notes

STEWED GREEN BEANS
with Tomatoes and Tarragon

THE KEY TO THIS SIMPLE DISH IS RIPE, SWEET TOMATOES (RIGHT OFF THE VINE IF POSSIBLE) AND CRISP, FRESH GREEN BEANS—FULL OF THE FLAVOR OF SUMMER. *If you have tomatoes with very thin skins, it's not even necessary to peel them. In fact, if you prefer, you can simply seed and chop the tomatoes. How easy is that?*

2 large tomatoes

1 pound green beans, stem ends trimmed

1 tablespoon unsalted butter

1 tablespoon extra-virgin olive oil

2 garlic cloves, thinly sliced

1½ teaspoons chopped fresh tarragon or ½ teaspoon dried

½ teaspoon salt

Set up a large bowl of ice and water.

Bring a medium pot of water to a boil. Add the tomatoes and cook for 10 seconds, until the skins loosen. Scoop them out with slotted spoon and transfer to the ice water. (Let the pot of water stay at the boil.) Peel the tomatoes, halve them, and squeeze out and discard the seeds. Chop the tomatoes.

In the same pot, cook the green beans until crisp-tender, about 3 minutes, then drain.

In a large skillet, heat the butter and oil over medium heat. Add the garlic and cook for 1 minute. Add the tomatoes, tarragon, and salt and cook until the tomatoes begin to thicken, about 5 minutes. Add the green beans and cook, tossing frequently, until the beans are tender and the sauce has thickened, 3 to 5 minutes.

Notes

BRAISED CUCUMBERS
with Dill

THIS RECIPE WAS ONE OF THOSE "WHO KNEW?" *discoveries that impresses our summer guests. Cucumbers become meltingly tender when cooked, with a flavor similar to that of yellow squash. Kirby cucumbers are crisp and unwaxed, allowing you to leave a little of the skin on to bring additional texture and color to the finished dish. Choose cucumbers that are not too large. The larger the cucumber, the seedier it tends to be.*

1½ tablespoons unsalted butter

1 leek, white and light green parts, diced and well washed (page 110)

6 Kirby cucumbers, peeled in stripes with a vegetable peeler, halved lengthwise, and cut crosswise into ½-inch slices

Salt

¼ cup chopped fresh dill

In a large skillet, melt 1 tablespoon of the butter over medium-low heat. Add the leek and cook, stirring occasionally, until tender, 3 to 5 minutes. Add the cucumbers, season with salt, and toss to coat.

Add ¼ cup water and the remaining ½ tablespoon butter, and cover the pan. Cook until the cucumbers are crisp-tender, about 3 minutes. Uncover the pan, increase the heat to medium, add the dill, and cook until the liquid has almost evaporated, 2 to 3 minutes.

Cucumbers

Although there are a host of cucumber varieties out there, the most common are the dark-green waxed cucumbers; the long, thin, often shrink-wrapped European cucumbers (also called English, burpless, seedless, or hothouse); and the smaller (3 to 6 inches), unwaxed Kirby cucumbers, the kind most often used for pickles. Armenian and Persian cucumbers, not as readily available, have thin, slightly bumpy, unwaxed skins and soft seeds—they're good for eating, not great for pickling.

Notes

Corn Chowder Salad

SOMETIMES DECONSTRUCTING A FAMILY RECIPE AND PUTTING IT BACK TOGETHER AGAIN IS INSPIRING. *All of a sudden a new classic is formed. Made with the ingredients you would find in a corn chowder, this salad is a burst of summer.*

2 teaspoons olive oil

3 slices bacon (about 2 ounces), cut crosswise into ½-inch pieces

½ pound Yukon Gold, red, or white boiling potatoes, peeled and cut into ½-inch dice

1 red bell pepper, cut into ½-inch squares

Salt

3 cups fresh corn kernels (from 6 ears)

1 small red onion, halved and thinly sliced

2 tablespoons cider vinegar or rice vinegar

Hot pepper flakes

In a large skillet, heat the oil over medium-low heat. Add the bacon and cook until crisp, about 5 minutes. With a slotted spoon, transfer the bacon to a paper towel to drain. Measure the fat remaining in the skillet; you need 2 tablespoons (if the bacon was particularly lean and you don't have enough, add olive oil to make up the difference).

Add the potatoes to the skillet and cook, tossing occasionally, until golden brown, about 5 minutes. Add the bell pepper, season with salt, and cook, tossing occasionally, until the pepper and potato are tender, about 5 minutes longer.

Add the corn and cook until piping hot, 3 to 5 minutes. Transfer to a bowl and add the onion, vinegar, and cooked bacon. Season with salt and hot pepper flakes and stir to combine. Serve warm, at room temperature, or chilled.

VARIATION When corn season is over, you can make this with 3 cups of frozen corn kernels.

Notes

Fried Green Tomatoes

THE GROWING SEASON AT THE BEEKMAN (WE'RE PRETTY FAR NORTH) IS TRAGICALLY SHORT, AND SOMETIMES THERE ARE TOMATOES THAT WE KNOW WILL JUST NEVER HAVE THE CHANCE TO RIPEN. *But waste not, want not. Fried green tomatoes are a part of Brent's southern childhood, but the absence of cornmeal in the pantry one day required a bit of improvisation. We tried them with panko bread crumbs and loved the extra crunch. The contrast of the crisp outer crust with the soft, tangy tomato underneath is wonderful and floods the mouth with memories of home.*

⅓ cup all-purpose flour

Salt

1 large egg

1 cup panko bread crumbs

2 to 3 tablespoons vegetable oil

1 pound green tomatoes, cut crosswise into ½-inch slices

In a wide shallow bowl or on a sheet of wax paper, stir together the flour and ½ teaspoon salt. In another shallow bowl, beat the egg with 1 tablespoon water. Place the panko in a separate bowl or on a sheet of wax paper.

Line a plate with paper towels. In a large skillet, heat 2 tablespoons of the oil over medium heat. Working in batches (however many slices will fit into the skillet in one layer), dip the tomato slices first in the flour, then in the egg, and finally in the panko, pressing so it adheres. Fry the tomatoes until golden brown and crisp, 2 to 3 minutes a side. Transfer to the paper towels. As you work, add up to 1 tablespoon more oil, if necessary, to prevent sticking. Sprinkle lightly with salt and serve hot.

Notes

ROASTED WHOLE BABY EGGPLANTS

SERVES 4

THESE SMALL, SWEET, RELATIVELY SEEDLESS EGGPLANTS ARE PERFECT FOR SINGLE SERVINGS—EACH PERSON GETS HIS OR HER OWN EGGPLANT.

¼ cup chopped fresh parsley

¼ cup chopped fresh basil leaves

2 tablespoons chopped fresh mint leaves

1 teaspoon grated lemon zest

1 tablespoon fresh lemon juice

3 garlic cloves, minced

½ teaspoon salt

3 tablespoons extra-virgin olive oil

4 baby eggplants (¼ pound each), halved lengthwise

Preheat the oven to 350°F. In a small bowl, combine the parsley, basil, mint, lemon zest, lemon juice, garlic, salt, and 2 tablespoons of the oil.

Make a V-shaped trench in the cut side of each eggplant half: with a paring knife held at an angle, starting about 1/2 inch from one end of the eggplant, make a cut down the center and to within 1/2 inch of the other end. Then with the knife held at the opposite angle, make another cut parallel to the first one, to make a V. Remove a wedge from the eggplant to leave a deep trench.

Fill the trench with the herb mixture and rub the cut surface with the remaining tablespoon of oil. Place 2 halves together, cut sides in. Wrap each eggplant in foil and place on a baking sheet.

Roast for 30 to 40 minutes, or until the eggplant is tender and can be easily pierced with the tip of a knife. Serve warm, at room temperature, or chilled.

VARIATIONS

• It's easy to grill eggplants, especially if you have the grill going for your main course. To grill the eggplants, preheat the grill to medium. Wrap the eggplant halves together as directed, and grill the packets, turning them over twice, until the package yields to gentle pressure.

• If you'd like a sauce to go with the eggplant, make a double batch of the herb-parsley mixture in step 1. Transfer half of the mixture to a small serving bowl and add 1 tablespoon of fresh lemon juice to it. Pass this sauce at the table. (Use the other half of the parsley mixture as directed.)

Notes

STEAMED EGGPLANT
with Herbed Goat Milk Yogurt

Notes

LONG, THIN JAPANESE EGGPLANTS TEND TO BE A LITTLE SWEETER THAN THE TRADITIONAL GLOBE ONES. *We like to peel eggplant, leaving some of the skin on in stripes. This helps to keep its shape, while lending texture and color. Steaming makes for quick cooking, and the flesh emerges creamy and tender.*

1 large Japanese eggplant (about ¾ pound), peeled lengthwise in stripes and cut crosswise into ½-inch slices

⅓ cup goat milk yogurt

2 teaspoons olive oil

½ teaspoon salt

2 tablespoons chopped dill

1 tablespoon chopped fresh mint leaves

In a steamer basket set over (not in) boiling water, cook the eggplant (it will be in more than one layer) until just tender but not falling apart, about 5 minutes.

Meanwhile, in a medium bowl, whisk together the yogurt, oil, and salt. Fold in the dill and mint. While the eggplant is still warm, add it to the yogurt mixture, tossing to coat. Refrigerate and serve chilled.

VARIATIONS

• You can also make this with cow milk yogurt.

• Try this with fresh basil instead of mint.

• To make this into a main-course salad: Steam the eggplant as directed. Double the yogurt dressing and also add 1 teaspoon grated lemon zest and a couple of teaspoons of fresh lemon juice (to taste). Add a can (15 ounces) of rinsed chickpeas to the dressing when you add the eggplant. Scatter ¼ cup chopped pistachios over the top.

Eggplant

There's no excuse for a lack of exoticism when it comes to eggplants. Landreth Seed Company sells fourteen varieties—from purple, to green, to striped, to white, to orange.

Quick Bread-and-Butter Pickles

MAKES 3 PINTS

THESE SWEET-TART PICKLES ARE QUICK TO MAKE—NO CANNING KETTLE REQUIRED—BUT THEY DO HAVE TO SIT OVERNIGHT BEFORE YOU CAN DIG IN. *We call them "refrigerator pickles" and love opening the fridge door and seeing a beautiful pickle jar full of them sitting on the top shelf. If you don't want to buy all the individual spices, pickling spice (found in the supermarket spice aisle) will be fine.*

6 medium Kirby cucumbers, ends trimmed, thinly sliced

1 small onion, halved and thinly sliced

2½ cups distilled white vinegar

¾ cup sugar

1 cinnamon stick, broken

4 teaspoons coarse salt

1 teaspoon yellow mustard seed

1 teaspoon coriander seed

1 teaspoon dill seed

½ teaspoon allspice berries

½ teaspoon black peppercorns

4 whole cloves

1 bay leaf, crumbled

In a large bowl, toss the cucumber slices with the onion.

In a medium saucepan, combine the vinegar, sugar, cinnamon, salt, mustard seed, coriander seed, dill seed, allspice, peppercorns, cloves, and bay leaf. Bring to a boil, reduce to a simmer, cover, and cook for 5 minutes.

Pour the hot spice mixture over the cucumber-onion mixture and place a piece of wax paper directly on the surface. Weight the mixture down with a plate. Let sit until totally cool.

Pack the cucumbers and the onions into three 1-pint glass canning jars. Pour the liquid and spices over the cucumbers, seal, and refrigerate overnight. (The cucumbers can be kept, refrigerated, for up to 3 months.)

VARIATION If you like a little heat, add a small fresh chile pepper to each jar.

Notes

Grandma's
POTATO SALAD

THIS IS THE KIND OF POTATO SALAD BRENT'S GRANDMA ALWAYS MADE— A SMOOTH MAYO-BASED SALAD PIQUANT WITH MUSTARD, CAPERS, AND PICKLES. *A mix of red, white, and blue potatoes makes the perfect salad to have on July Fourth, but you could just use yellow potatoes, such as Yukon Gold.*

½ pound small red potatoes

½ pound small white potatoes

½ pound small blue potatoes

2 large eggs

⅓ cup mayonnaise

1 tablespoon brown mustard

2 teaspoons cider vinegar

¾ teaspoon salt

1 dill pickle, cut into small dice

2 tablespoons capers, rinsed

Place the potatoes in a medium saucepan with cold salted water to cover. Bring to a boil, reduce to a simmer, and cook until the potatoes can be pierced with the tip of a knife, about 20 minutes (timing will vary depending on the size of the potatoes).

Meanwhile, place the eggs in a medium saucepan with cold water to cover by several inches. Bring to a boil. Remove from the heat, cover, and let the eggs stand for 12 minutes. Transfer to a bowl of ice water. Peel the eggs. Halve the eggs lengthwise and thickly slice.

In a large bowl, whisk together the mayonnaise, mustard, vinegar, and salt.

When the potatoes are cool enough to handle but still warm, peel them if you like and then cut into ½-inch-thick slices. Add to the mayonnaise dressing and toss gently to combine. Fold in the eggs, pickle, and capers. Let cool to room temperature; then chill for at least 1 hour before serving.

VARIATIONS

• Use a spicy mustard instead of brown, and add 1 tablespoon drained horseradish.

• To make this into a main course, add ½ pound ham, diced, and 1 red bell pepper, diced. For the dressing, increase the vinegar by 2 teaspoons and increase the mayo by 1 tablespoon.

Notes

SOUR CHERRY CLAFOUTI

SOUR CHERRIES, SOMETIMES CALLED PIE CHERRIES, HAVE A VERY SHORT
SEASON (LATE JUNE INTO JULY), AND WE RACE TO PICK THEM BEFORE
THE BIRDS DO, SO WE CAN WHIP UP THIS TRADITIONAL FRENCH COUNTRY
DESSERT—A CROSS BETWEEN A TART AND A PANCAKE. *If you miss the fresh*
sour cherry season, you can get water- or syrup-packed sour cherries in jars
(drain before using).

1 tablespoon unsalted butter

1¼ pounds sour cherries, pitted

½ cup all-purpose flour

1 cup milk

½ cup heavy cream

⅓ cup plus 2 tablespoons sugar

1 tablespoon kirsch (cherry brandy) or
2 teaspoons pure vanilla extract

3 large eggs

Preheat the oven to 350°F. Use the butter to grease a 9-inch pie plate.

Place the cherries in the pie plate. Put the flour in a large bowl. Whisk the
milk into the flour until smooth, then whisk in the cream, ⅓ cup of the sugar,
the kirsch, and the eggs until well combined. Pour the batter over the cherries.
Sprinkle the top with the remaining 2 tablespoons sugar and bake for
45 minutes, or until set. Let cool slightly on a rack and serve warm. (The
clafouti will fall as it cools.)

VARIATION Substitute sweet cherries for the sour cherries and reduce the
sugar to ¼ cup plus 2 tablespoons.

Notes

SOUR CHERRY SORBET

1 pound sour cherries, pitted

1½ cups sugar

1 cup water

1½ teaspoons freshly ground black pepper

Puree the cherries in a food processor until smooth. In a medium saucepan combine the puree and remaining ingredients. Bring the mixture to a boil, then reduce the heat and simmer for 5 minutes. Strain the mixture through a fine-mesh sieve into a bowl and refrigerate until cold, at least 4 hours or overnight.

Make the sorbet in an ice cream machine according to manufacturer's directions.

VARIATION You can substitute raspberries for the sour cherries.

Notes

BUTTERY PEACH CAKE

THIS SUPEREASY CAKE, DOLLED UP WITH A LITTLE AROMATIC CARDAMOM AND GINGER, IS THE PERFECT LITTLE BLACK DRESS FOR SWEET PEACHES. *If you have a choice, pick freestone peaches, as it will be easier to remove their pits. Once the cake has cooled, pull up some chairs, grab a pitcher of cold milk and a few spoons, and serve the cake right out of the pan.*

PEACHES

1½ pounds peaches

2 tablespoons unsalted butter, melted

3 tablespoons sugar

½ teaspoon ground ginger

½ teaspoon ground cardamom

CAKE

1¼ cups all-purpose flour, spooned and leveled (page 165)

1 teaspoon baking powder

¼ teaspoon baking soda

¼ teaspoon salt

4 tablespoons (½ stick) unsalted butter, softened

¾ cup plus 1 tablespoon sugar

2 large eggs, separated

1 teaspoon pure vanilla extract

⅓ cup plain whole-milk yogurt

Preheat the oven to 350°F. Grease a 9-inch square baking pan.

FOR THE PEACHES Bring a large pot of water to a boil. Set up a large bowl with ice and water. Drop the peaches one at a time into the boiling water and boil for 30 seconds. With a slotted spoon, transfer the peaches to the ice water to cool. With either your fingers or a paring knife, peel off and discard the skin. Cut the peaches into 1/2-inch-thick slices and transfer to a bowl.

Add the melted butter, sugar, ginger, and cardamom and toss to coat. Transfer to the baking pan.

FOR THE CAKE In a medium bowl, whisk together the flour, baking powder, baking soda, and salt. With a mixer, beat the butter and ¾ cup of the sugar until light and fluffy. Beat in the egg yolks and vanilla until well combined. Alternately add the flour mixture and the yogurt to the batter, beginning and ending with the flour mixture, beating until just combined.

In a separate bowl, beat the egg whites until foamy. Beat in the remaining 1 tablespoon sugar until stiff peaks form. Gently fold the whites into the batter. Scrape the batter over the peaches.

Bake for 35 minutes, or until the top is lightly browned and the fruit has risen close to the top. Let cool in the pan, and serve at room temperature.

VARIATIONS

- Deep black plums are delicious here. Substitute for half the peaches or make the cake with all plums.
- Use 3 cups pitted cherries instead of peaches. Omit the ginger and add 1/8 teaspoon almond extract to the fruit.

Buying Peaches

Chances are, you'll find freestone peaches in your market. As the name implies, these peaches have a pit that is easily removed. Clingstone peaces, usually used commercially, have a pit that clings to the peach; so avoid using them.

To ripen hard peaches, place them in a brown paper bag on the kitchen counter where they'll ripen in a few days.

DOUBLE BLUEBERRY TART

COOKED BLUEBERRIES WITH THEIR JAMLIKE FLAVOR AND TEXTURE ARE CONTRASTED HERE WITH THE TART INTENSITY AND SLIGHT CRUNCH OF FRESH BLUEBERRIES. *A little bit of fresh black pepper is a nice counterpoint to the sweetness of the berries. Wonderful as a dessert or as an indulgent treat for Sunday brunch.*

Basic Pie Dough (page 27)

6 cups blueberries

1 teaspoon grated lemon zest

¼ cup fresh lemon juice

⅔ cup sugar

3 tablespoons cornstarch

½ teaspoon ground cinnamon

¼ teaspoon freshly ground black pepper

Sweetened whipped cream (optional)

On a lightly floured work surface, roll the dough out to a 12-inch round. Fit the dough into a 9-inch tart pan with a removable bottom; trim excess dough. Form a high border and flute the edge. Refrigerate for 30 minutes.

Preheat the oven to 400°F. Line the dough with a sheet of foil and weight the foil down with dried beans, rice, or pie weights. Place the tart pan on a baking sheet and bake for 10 minutes to set the sides. Carefully remove the foil and the weights and bake for 10 to 12 minutes longer, or until the pastry is golden and baked through. If any air bubbles appear as the shell is baking, prick them gently with a fork. Cool the shell in the pan on a rack.

In a medium, heavy-bottomed saucepan, combine 2 cups of the berries, the lemon zest, the lemon juice, and 2 tablespoons of water. In a small bowl, stir together the sugar, cornstarch, cinnamon, and pepper. Add to the berry mixture and stir to coat. Cook over medium heat, stirring constantly, until the mixture comes to a boil and thickens, 1 to 2 minutes. Transfer to a bowl, place a sheet of wax paper directly on the surface, and let cool to room temperature.

Stir 3 cups of the fresh berries into the cooked blueberries and spoon into the baked shell. Scatter the remaining 1 cup fresh berries over the top. If you like, serve with whipped cream.

Notes

Jumble Berry Pie

A JUMBLE OF SUMMER BERRIES—BLUEBERRIES, RASPBERRIES, AND BLACKBERRIES—IS TOSSED WITH QUICK-COOKING TAPIOCA AND CORNSTARCH, WHICH TURN THE DELICIOUS BERRY JUICES INTO A SAUCE FOR THE FRUIT.

Double recipe Basic Pie Dough (page 27)

1⅓ cups sugar

3 tablespoons cornstarch

2 tablespoons quick-cooking tapioca

½ teaspoon ground cinnamon

¼ teaspoon salt

⅛ teaspoon ground allspice

3 cups blueberries

2 cups raspberries

2 cups blackberries

1 teaspoon grated orange zest

1 tablespoon unsalted butter, cut into bits

¼ cup heavy cream

Follow the recipe for Basic Pie Dough, doubling all of the ingredients. Form the dough into two discs. Wrap separately in wax paper or plastic wrap and refrigerate for at least 1 hour.

Preheat the oven to 400°F

On a lightly floured work surface, roll out one disc of the dough to a 12-inch round. Roll the dough around the rolling pin and transfer it to a 9-inch deep-dish pie plate, fitting it in without stretching it. Press the dough into the bottom and sides of the pan. With a pair of scissors or a paring knife, trim the top of the dough to form a 1-inch overhang. Refrigerate while you make the filling.

In a large bowl, whisk together the sugar, cornstarch, tapioca, cinnamon, salt, and allspice. Add the berries and orange zest and toss to coat.

On a lightly floured work surface, roll out the second disc of dough to a 13-inch round. Pile the berry filling into the pastry-lined pie plate, scraping any of the cornstarch-spice mixture left in the bowl over the berries. Dot the berries with the butter.

Fit the second dough round over the berries, trimming it to a 1-inch overhang. Pinch the two overhangs together, fold up, and with your fingers, crimp to make a high fluted edge.

Notes

Brush the crust with the cream and make several slashes in the top for steam vents. Place the pie on a rimmed baking sheet and bake for 15 minutes.

Reduce the oven temperature to 350°F and bake for 45 minutes, or until the juices are bubbling and thick. If the crust is browning too much before the pie is done, tent the pie with foil.

Cool on a rack for at least 4 hours before serving.

VARIATIONS

- Use lemon zest instead of orange zest and add 1 teaspoon pure vanilla extract to the berry mix.
- Though we are not personally fans of cooked strawberries, many people are. Just be sure to cut them up into smaller, berry-sized chunks before using them, and mix them with other berries that have more body. Try this mix: 2 cups strawberries, 3 cups blueberries, 2 cups blackberries.
- To give the berries a little zing, add ½ teaspoon freshly ground black pepper to the berry mix along with ⅛ teaspoon ground cloves.

Zesters

A Microplane zester, a tool that resembles a wood file, is particularly useful in getting the most zest off the lemons and oranges. The zest, the colored layer of the peel (not the spongy, bitter pith that lies underneath), gives a tangy bite and helps round out the flavors of a dish.

Raspberries

One of the first things we did after moving into the Beekman was to walk around the property debating where to put our vegetable garden. As we were trudging through the weeds on the east side of the barn we stumbled on a scraggly row of raspberry bushes (ouch). Those old bushes still put out dozens and dozens of quarts of bright red berries each summer and fall. Now we've lengthened the row by adding several more varieties. We transplanted some wild Black Caps from the edge of our woods that make an exotically dark jelly; supersweet and juicy Royalty Purple Raspberries; winter-hardy Triple Crown Blackberries; and our favorite, Anne Golden Raspberries—whose yellow color hints at its almost-pineapple overtones.

To store raspberries, we freeze them immediately after picking. There's no reason to wash them if they haven't been treated with pesticides. We spread ours out on a baking sheet and place the sheet in the freezer overnight. Once the berries are solidly frozen, they can be transferred to a freezer bag.

For man, autumn is a time of harvest, of gathering together. For nature, it is a time of sowing, of scattering abroad.

—EDWIN WAY TEALE

FALL

fter the feverish heat and delirious fervor of summer, autumn is a welcome respite. Prior months were spent fighting back all the forces of Mother Nature, but now we lay down our weed-whacking and bug-swatting weaponry and concede defeat. She ultimately always wins, and her victory reminds us that everything in life has a season. It must.

Perhaps that is why autumn inspires so many cornucopias of gratitude.

A memory from Brent's childhood: After the Thanksgiving Day meal (always a late lunch rather than a dinner), the table and all of the food still on it would be covered with a crisp white sheet. The whole family would then go for a walk in the deep woods that surrounded the house. After several miles of leaves crunching beneath our feet, we'd return home, inhale the earthy aroma of new logs thrown into the woodstove, uncover the table, and eat again.

Continue ☞

Cheese Toast-Topped

ONION SOUP

IT ALWAYS SEEMS THAT THE FIRST THING TO COME OUT OF THE ROOT CELLAR EACH AUTUMN (EVEN THOUGH THEY'VE BEEN HANGING FOR ONLY A FEW WEEKS) IS A BUNDLE OF ONIONS FOR A SLOWLY COOKED POT OF ONION SOUP—THE PERFECT HERALD TO THE SEASON. *This richly flavored soup—with sweet, golden onions, red wine, and just a touch of sherry—is made even more irresistible with a topping of country bread and melted cheese.*

2 tablespoons extra-virgin olive oil

2 tablespoons unsalted butter

2½ pounds large yellow onions, halved, peeled, and thinly sliced (8 cups)

4 sprigs fresh thyme or ¾ teaspoon dried

¾ cup red wine

2 tablespoons sherry

6 cups Chicken Stock (page 17) or reduced-sodium canned broth

1 teaspoon salt

Freshly ground black pepper

8 slices crusty country bread

¼ pound Blaak cheese (page 130) or Gruyère cheese, thinly sliced

In a 5-quart Dutch oven, heat the oil and butter over medium-low heat. Add the onions and thyme, cover, and cook, stirring occasionally, until the onions are soft, about 20 minutes. Uncover and cook, stirring frequently, until golden brown, about 25 minutes.

Stir in the red wine and sherry, scraping up any browned bits from the bottom of the pan. Add the stock, salt, and pepper to taste. Bring to a boil, reduce to a simmer, and cook for 30 minutes to concentrate the flavors.

Preheat the broiler.

Divide the soup among 8 soup bowls. Cut each slice of bread in half and place on a baking sheet or broiler pan. Top with the cheese. Broil the cheese toasts 4 to 6 inches from the heat for 2 minutes, or until the cheese has melted. Place 2 slices in each bowl of soup.

Notes

ROASTED CAULIFLOWER AND APPLE SOUP

Notes

IF YOU GREW UP EATING CAULIFLOWER THAT WAS BOILED TO DEATH AND CAN'T IMAGINE WHY ANYONE WOULD WANT TO EAT IT, WE GUARANTEE THIS DISH WILL CHANGE YOUR MIND. *Roasting caramelizes the natural sugars in the cauliflower and intensifies its flavor—boiling does pretty much the opposite. The silky smoothness of this soup may fool you into thinking it has cream in it, but there's not even a smidgen. The trick is to use a blender. While a food processor is good for many things, a blender is the perfect tool to use when you want a soup with a creamy texture.*

1 head cauliflower (about 2 pounds)

2 sweet apples, such as Crispin or Northern Spy (¾ pound total), peeled and cut into 1-inch chunks

1 onion, cut into 8 chunks

¼ cup sliced fresh ginger

3 garlic cloves, peeled

Salt

3 tablespoons extra-virgin olive oil

5 cups Chicken Stock (page 17) or reduced-sodium canned chicken broth or vegetable broth

Grated nutmeg, for garnish

Preheat the oven to 425°F. Cut off and discard the very tough bottom of the cauliflower. Halve the cauliflower lengthwise; then cut crosswise into ½-inch-thick slices (including the central stalk). Transfer to a roasting pan along with the apples, onion, ginger, garlic, and ½ teaspoon of salt. Add the oil and toss to coat.

Roast for 40 minutes, tossing the vegetables occasionally, until the cauliflower is lightly browned and the onion is tender.

Working in batches, transfer some of the vegetable mixture and some of the broth to a blender (don't fill the blender more than half full for each batch). Puree until very smooth, 3 to 4 minutes. As you work, transfer the puree to a saucepan.

Place the saucepan over low heat to reheat the puree. Add salt to taste. Serve garnished with a grating of nutmeg.

BROCCOLI-CHEDDAR SOUP

WE LIKE TO USE AS MANY PARTS OF THE VEGETABLE AS POSSIBLE, AND SOMETIMES WE FIND THE TRUE ESSENCE IN THE PARTS OF THE PLANT THAT ARE LESS OFTEN USED. *Both the broccoli stalk and the florets are used in this creamy soup rich with cheese. The stalks are very sweet; all they need is a little peeling to make them edible. A small amount of cayenne gives the soup a little heat. If you like, garnish the soup with croutons (see Dandelion Salad with Slab Bacon, Croutons, and Hot Bacon Dressing, page 8).*

1 tablespoon unsalted butter

1 medium onion, chopped

2 tablespoons long-grain white rice

2 cups vegetable or chicken broth

1 head broccoli (1 pound), end trimmed

2 cups milk

2 cups (8 ounces) shredded sharp Cheddar cheese

¾ teaspoon salt

⅛ teaspoon cayenne pepper

In a large saucepan, melt the butter over medium heat. Add the onion and cook, stirring frequently, until the onion is tender, about 5 minutes. Stir in the rice, add the broth, and simmer until the rice is tender, 12 to 15 minutes.

Separate the broccoli florets from the stalk. Peel the stalk and thinly slice. Coarsely chop the florets.

Add the milk to the onion and rice mixture along with the sliced broccoli stalk and cook 4 minutes. Add the florets and cook until still bright green but tender, about 4 minutes longer. Remove the pan from the heat.

If you have an immersion blender, use it to puree the soup right in the pot until smooth. If not, working in batches, transfer the mixture to a food processor or blender and puree until smooth (use caution when blending hot liquids). Return to the pot and reheat.

Remove the pan from the heat, add the cheese, salt, and cayenne, and stir until the cheese has melted.

Notes

ROASTED BEET AND GOAT CHEESE SALAD

Notes

EVEN THOUGH JOSH DOESN'T CARE SO MUCH FOR BEETS, HE LOVES TO GROW BOTH RED AND GOLDEN VARIETIES, AND THEY OFTEN FIND THEIR WAY INTO THIS BEAUTIFUL SALAD, WHICH ALWAYS GETS RAVES. *Roasting the beets intensifies their sweet flavor, and though the cooking may take a long time, it's definitely worth the wait. Caramelizing the pecans is really quite easy, so while you're at it, make a big batch of these nuts and keep them on hand for adding to other dishes—they'll keep about a week at room temperature, packed in an airtight container.*

6 beets (3 red, 3 golden), tops removed and reserved for another use (see Cooking Greens, page 138)

1 tablespoon sugar

1 teaspoon ground coriander

Salt

⅓ cup pecans

3 tablespoons fresh lemon juice

3 tablespoons extra-virgin olive oil

1 teaspoon Dijon mustard

3 Kirby cucumbers, peeled and thinly sliced

1 fennel bulb, halved lengthwise and thinly sliced crosswise

1 bunch arugula

4 to 6 ounces soft goat cheese, crumbled

Preheat the oven to 425°F. Rinse the beets and wrap in foil (if they are of a similar size, you can wrap several together). Place on a baking sheet and bake for 1 to 1¼ hours, or until the beets yield to gentle pressure. When cool enough to handle, unwrap and slip the skins off (use a paper towel or kitchen gloves so you don't stain your hands). Cut the beets in half and thinly slice.

Meanwhile, in a small skillet, combine the sugar, coriander, and ¼ teaspoon salt. Add the pecans and cook over low heat, tossing occasionally, until the sugar has melted and is lightly caramelized (the color of a brown paper bag), about 5 minutes. Immediately transfer the nuts to a plate to stop further cooking and darkening of the sugar.

In a large bowl, whisk together the lemon juice, oil, and mustard. Season with salt to taste. Add the beets, cucumbers, fennel, arugula, and pecans and toss to combine. Serve with the goat cheese scattered over the top.

MULLED CIDER

Notes

EVERY YEAR AFTER WE PRESS OUR APPLES—A FULL-DAY PROCESS THAT STARTS WITH THE PICKING EARLY IN THE MORNING—WE CELEBRATE WITH NEIGHBORS BY TOASTING THE SEASON WITH A CUP OF MULLED CIDER. *It's sweet, spicy, and piquant from the fresh ginger. A little maple syrup added at the end makes for a smooth beverage.*

1 quart apple cider

1 cinnamon stick, halved lengthwise

1 (2-inch) piece fresh ginger, thinly sliced

Zest strips from ½ orange

8 whole cloves

5 allspice berries

3 tablespoons maple syrup (preferably grade B)

In a medium saucepan, combine the cider, cinnamon, ginger, orange zest, cloves, and allspice. Bring the mixture to a boil, reduce to a simmer, cover, and cook for 5 minutes. Strain the mixture and discard the spices. Return the mixture to a gentle simmer and stir in the maple syrup. Serve warm.

VARIATION For a "grown-up" mulled cider, add ¼ cup applejack, dark rum, or bourbon to the cider after it's been heated.

Red Wine and Spice

POACHED PEARS

THERE'S SOMETHING BOTH HOMEY AND ELEGANT ABOUT POACHED PEARS, AND WHILE THEY CAN BE POACHED IN ANY TYPE OF WINE, OR EVEN JUICE, WE'RE PARTICULARLY FOND OF RED WINE BECAUSE OF THE DEEP PURPLE COLOR IT LENDS TO THE PEARS. *Bosc pears, because their texture is firm and dense, are perfect for poaching: They can cook for a long time, absorbing the flavors without falling apart.*

4 firm-ripe Bosc pears (about 2½ pounds total), stem on if possible

1 bottle dry red wine, such as Shiraz

⅔ cup sugar

1 vanilla bean, split lengthwise

8 allspice berries

8 black peppercorns

1 cinnamon stick

With a melon baller or small sturdy measuring spoon, core the pears from the bottom. Peel the pears.

In a saucepan large enough to hold the pears (lying on their sides) in a single layer, combine the wine, sugar, vanilla bean, allspice, peppercorns, and cinnamon stick. Add the pears. Cut a round of wax paper large enough to cover the pears, and place it on top of them. Bring to a simmer, cover, and cook for 30 minutes.

Carefully turn the pears over and cook until the pears can be pierced with a paring knife but still hold their shape and are not falling apart, about 30 minutes longer. Transfer the pears to a shallow bowl.

Bring the wine mixture to a boil over high heat and cook until reduced to 1 cup with the consistency of a thick syrup, about 10 minutes. Cool the syrup and pour over the pears. (The pears can be kept in the refrigerator covered by their syrup for several days.)

VARIATION The pears can be stuffed with a soft cheese, such as goat cheese or blue cheese (Roquefort or Danish blue).

Notes

CHICKEN WITH SUCCOTASH

SUCCOTASH, A SIDE DISH OF SHELL BEANS (TYPICALLY LIMAS) AND CORN, IS POPULAR IN THE SOUTH. *Brent's grandmother Jewel brought it to every family meal. Lima beans are a love 'em or hate 'em vegetable, and who knows why. Cooked here, along with chicken, in a broth scented with thyme and a dash of smoky, not hot, ancho chile powder, lima beans achieve the top position they deserve. Add the corn at the last minute, as it requires just a little heating up; too long on the stove and it loses some of its sweetness.*

2 tomatoes

2 tablespoons extra-virgin olive oil

1 whole chicken (about 3 pounds), cut into 8 pieces

1 small onion, finely chopped

1 small green bell pepper, cut into ½-inch squares

1 cup fresh shelled or frozen lima beans

1 cup Chicken Stock (page 17) or reduced-sodium canned broth

¾ teaspoon salt

½ teaspoon dried thyme

½ teaspoon ancho chile powder

2 cups fresh or frozen corn kernels

Chopped parsley (optional)

Bring a pot of water to a boil. Add the tomatoes and cook for 10 seconds, until the skins loosen. When cool enough to handle, peel and coarsely chop.

In a 5-quart Dutch oven, heat the oil over medium heat. Add the chicken and cook until golden brown, flipping the chicken over once, about 5 minutes per side. Transfer to a bowl.

Add the onion and bell pepper to the pan and cook, stirring frequently, until the onion is tender, about 7 minutes.

Add the tomatoes to the pan with the onion and pepper.

Add the lima beans, chicken stock, salt, thyme, and chile powder and bring to a boil. Return the chicken to the pan, reduce to a simmer, cover, and cook until the lima beans are tender and the chicken is cooked through, about 20 minutes.

Stir in the corn and simmer until just cooked, about 2 minutes. Serve sprinkled with parsley, if desired.

Notes

BEER-BRAISED BEEF

with Onion Dumplings

A DRIVE TO THE BREWERY OMMEGANG JUST A FEW MILES FROM THE FARM INSPIRED THIS HEARTY DISH THAT IS ALWAYS ENJOYED WHEN JOSH'S PARENTS COME TO VISIT. *Choose a rich dark beer for this dish, one that's full flavored and robust. During the final phase of the cooking, when you've added the dumplings, cook the stew on top of the stove. The tops of the dumplings will be dry, while the undersides will be moist with the stew juices.*

·⋅[BEEF]⋅·

4 tablespoons vegetable oil

3 pounds boneless chuck (fatty rather than lean), cut into 1½-inch chunks

¼ cup all-purpose flour

2 pounds onions, coarsely chopped

½ pound carrots, thickly sliced

3 garlic cloves, smashed and peeled

½ teaspoon dried thyme

¼ teaspoon ground allspice

⅛ teaspoon ground cloves

1 bottle (12 ounces) dark beer

1 tablespoon tomato paste

1 teaspoon salt

·⋅[DUMPLINGS]⋅·

6 tablespoons unsalted butter, melted

⅓ cup finely chopped onion

½ cup buttermilk

2 tablespoons chopped fresh dill

1 cup all-purpose flour

1 teaspoon baking powder

½ teaspoon baking soda

¼ teaspoon salt

½ cup fine fresh bread crumbs

FOR THE BEEF Preheat the oven to 350°F. In a 5- to 7-quart Dutch oven or heavy-bottomed saucepan, heat 2 tablespoons of the oil over medium-high heat. Dredge the beef in the flour, shaking off the excess. Working in batches (this is so the meat browns, rather than steams), cook the meat until browned all over, about 5 minutes. Transfer the meat to a bowl.

Add the remaining 2 tablespoons oil to the pan along with the onions, carrots, and garlic. Reduce the heat to medium, cover, and cook, stirring occasionally, until the vegetables are crisp-tender, 12 to 15 minutes. Stir in the thyme, allspice, cloves, beer, tomato paste, salt, and 2 cups water and bring to a boil.

Return the meat to the pan. Cover and place in the oven. Bake for
1½ hours, or until the meat is tender. Place the pan on the stovetop.

MEANWHILE, FOR THE DUMPLINGS In a small skillet, heat 1 tablespoon of the
melted butter. Add the onion and cook until tender, about 5 minutes. Transfer
to a small bowl and stir in the buttermilk, dill, and 2 tablespoons of the melted
butter. In a medium bowl, whisk together the flour, baking powder, baking soda,
and salt. Make a well in the center of the flour mixture and add the buttermilk
mixture. Stir the dumpling mixture gently until moistened.

In a shallow bowl, stir the remaining 3 tablespoons melted butter into the
bread crumbs. One at a time, drop the dumpling mixture by rounded tablespoon
into the crumb mixture and turn to coat with the crumbs. (You should end up
with 12 dumplings.)

Drop the dumplings onto the simmering stew, spacing them evenly. Cover
the pan and simmer the stew until the dumplings are tender and cooked
through, about 20 minutes.

Onions

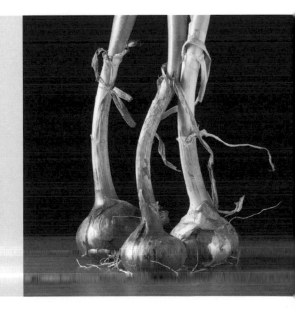

We grow several varieties of onions in our garden: white, yellow, red, and
shallots. White onions are best used in stews and boiled dishes, yellow onions
are generally best for sautéing, and red onions are our favorite when used raw.
Shallots are often called "the chef's secret" due to their sweet flavor and slight
garlic overtones.

There are as many different onion-cutting techniques as there are cooking
schools, but the most important tip of all is to always cut the onion in half first,
then finish chopping with the cut side firmly facedown on the chopping board.
Countless fingertips have been saved by this method.

SERVES 4

Butternut Squash–Filled
LASAGNA ROLLS

PARMESAN, SWEET SQUASH, ALMONDS, SAGE, AND A HINT OF SUGAR ARE THE FLAVORS IN A CLASSIC TORTELLINI OR RAVIOLI FILLING. *Here the mixture is used to stuff rolled-up lasagna noodles, which are baked in a simple mixture of cream and Parmesan.*

2 pounds butternut squash	1 tablespoon Dijon mustard
8 lasagna noodles	2 teaspoons light brown sugar
1⅓ cups grated Parmesan cheese	1 teaspoon finely chopped fresh sage or ½ teaspoon dried
1 large egg	
¼ cup natural (unblanched) almonds, finely ground	½ teaspoon salt
	½ teaspoon freshly ground black pepper
¼ cup panko bread crumbs	¾ cup heavy cream

Preheat the oven to 400°F.

Halve the squash crosswise, separating the narrow neck from the bulbous bottom. Cut them both in half lengthwise; scoop out and discard the seeds. Place the squash on a rimmed baking sheet, cut side down, cover with foil, and bake for 45 minutes, or until the squash is tender. (Leave the oven on.) Scoop out the flesh of the squash and mash. Measure out 1½ cups and freeze the remainder for another use.

Grease a 9-inch square baking dish.

In a large pot of boiling salted water, cook the noodles according to package directions. Drain and run under cold water.

In a medium bowl, stir together the squash puree, ⅔ cup of the Parmesan, the egg, almonds, panko, mustard, brown sugar, sage, salt, and pepper. Place the lasagna noodles on a work surface with the short ends facing you. Spread the squash mixture over each noodle. Roll the noodles up into compact bundles and place them, seam side down, in the baking dish.

Pour the cream over the noodles and sprinkle the remaining ⅔ cup Parmesan over the top. Bake for 25 minutes, or until the cream is bubbling and the top of the dish is lightly browned.

Notes

BLUE CHEESE PIZZA
with Caramelized Onion

SERVES 4

BRENT HAS NEVER MET A PIZZA HE DIDN'T LIKE. *Josh's tastes are a little more eclectic. Here's the compromise: blue cheese, a little apple, walnuts, and sweet caramelized onions. Choose any pizza dough—white or whole wheat—and make sure you get your oven nice and hot before you pop it in the pizza.*

6 tablespoons extra-virgin olive oil

2½ pounds onions, halved and thinly sliced

1 large sweet apple, peeled and cut into thin wedges

Salt

¾ pound store-bought or homemade pizza dough

8 ounces blue cheese, crumbled

⅓ cup walnuts, coarsely chopped

In a large skillet, heat 4 tablespoons of the oil over low heat. Add the onions, cover, and cook, stirring occasionally, until tender, about 25 minutes.

Uncover the onions and continue cooking, stirring frequently, until golden brown, about 20 minutes. Stir in the apple, season with salt to taste, and cook until the apple is crisp-tender, about 5 minutes.

Preheat the oven to 500°F with a rack set in the lowest position.

On a lightly floured work surface, roll the dough out to a 14-inch round. Transfer the dough to a large baking sheet and brush the top with the remaining 2 tablespoons oil. Scatter the caramelized onion-apple mixture over the top, leaving a 1-inch border all around. Scatter the cheese and nuts on top. Bake for 12 to 15 minutes, or until the crust is crisp and the cheese has melted.

Notes

HARVEST BEEF CHILI
with Pumpkin and Beans

AT HARVESTTIME—WHEN THE PUMPKINS ARE READY TO BE MOVED FROM THE FIELDS TO THE KITCHENS—THE WEATHER IS GETTING A LITTLE NIPPY. *What could be more perfect than a bowl of nice hot chili? Choose whatever cooking pumpkin or winter squash you like for this stew. We're particularly fond of kabocha, a sweet winter squash with a texture reminiscent of chestnuts. The skin is perfectly edible, so if you prefer, leave it on.*

Notes

3 tablespoons extra-virgin olive oil

1¼ pounds well-marbled beef chuck, cut into 1-inch chunks

¼ cup flour

1 large onion, diced

1 red bell pepper, cut into 1-inch chunks

3 garlic cloves, smashed and peeled

1½ teaspoons ground coriander

1 teaspoon ground cumin

1 teaspoon paprika

1 teaspoon unsweetened cocoa powder

½ teaspoon ancho chile powder

2 tablespoons tomato paste

1½ pounds pumpkin (or other winter squash, such as kabocha), peeled, seeded, and cut into 1-inch chunks

1½ teaspoons salt

1¾ cups cooked pinto beans or 1 can (15 ounces), rinsed

Preheat the oven to 350°F.

In a 5- or 6-quart Dutch oven, heat the oil over medium heat. Dredge the meat in the flour, shaking off the excess. Working in batches (this is so the meat browns, rather than steams), add the beef and cook until browned all over, about 7 minutes. As you work, transfer the meat to a bowl.

Add the onion, bell pepper, and garlic to the pan and stir to coat. Cook for 5 minutes, stirring frequently. Add ¼ cup water and cook, stirring occasionally, until the onion is tender, about 7 minutes.

Stir in the coriander, cumin, paprika, cocoa powder, and ancho chile powder. Return the meat to the pan and stir until well coated. Stir in 1½ cups water, the tomato paste, pumpkin, and salt. Bring to a boil. Cover and transfer to the oven. Bake for 1½ hours, or until the meat is tender.

Stir in the beans, return to the oven, and bake for 10 more minutes.

Recipe continues

Pumpkins are one of the oldest garden plants grown in America, and we have the Native Americans to thank for them. Pumpkins—there's just something about them that makes us smile.

One season, we planted our pumpkins and promptly forgot about them. It wasn't until about three months after we planted them that we started poking around in the patch to see if any had set fruit. We lifted up one large leaf and actually startled ourselves. There lay a gigantic King of Mammoth pumpkin . . . already about 20 pounds or so. (They can get as big as 250 pounds!) By the time fall came, it looked like the ground had been bombarded by a meteor shower of pumpkins.

VARIATIONS

- Once the stew is finished cooking, add enough broth to make it soupy. Stir in a 10-ounce package of frozen corn kernels and a couple of handfuls of toasted tortilla chips. Serve with hot sauce on the side.
- Use pork shoulder instead of beef and black beans instead of pinto beans. Swap in a green bell pepper for the red and serve with lime wedges and chopped cilantro on the side.

Stew Beef

The difference between a tender beef stew and a tough one has to do with the cut of meat. Although shopping for the beef can be a bit tricky, it doesn't have to be. Simply look for chuck, a cut that is well marbled, with veins of fat that melt during cooking and render the meat moist and tender. Don't be fooled into buying something called "stew meat," because you'll have no way of knowing what cut or cuts of beef you are buying. You also should stay away from cuts called "top round" or "bottom round" (even though many recipes call for it), because it is too lean to end up tender when it's cooked.

SAUTÉED CHICKEN
with Pears

SERVES 4

PEARS, RED WINE, AND A SMIDGE OF SWEET-TART BALSAMIC VINEGAR MAKE THIS QUICK WEEKNIGHT DINNER ELEGANT. *Rosemary and thyme add a slightly herbal note that works with both the sauce and the pears. A swirl of butter at the end gives the sauce a little body and creaminess.*

1 tablespoon plus 2 teaspoons vegetable oil

4 skinless, boneless chicken breast halves (6 to 8 ounces each)

2 tablespoons all-purpose flour

1 pound Bartlett pears, peeled, halved lengthwise, and thickly sliced crosswise

⅓ cup dry red wine

½ cup Chicken Stock (page 17) or reduced-sodium canned broth

1 tablespoon balsamic vinegar

½ teaspoon salt

¼ teaspoon dried rosemary, crumbled

¼ teaspoon dried thyme, crumbled

⅛ teaspoon freshly ground black pepper

1 tablespoon cold unsalted butter

In a large skillet, heat 1 tablespoon of the oil over medium heat. Dredge the chicken in the flour. Add to the skillet and cook until golden brown, about 3 minutes per side. Transfer to a plate.

Add the remaining 2 teaspoons oil to the pan along with the pears. Cook until lightly browned, about 4 minutes. Add the wine, bring to a boil, and cook for 2 minutes. Add the stock, vinegar, salt, rosemary, thyme, and pepper. Return the chicken (and any juices from the plate) to the skillet and simmer until the chicken is cooked through, about 5 minutes.

Transfer the chicken and pears to a platter. Remove the pan from the heat, add the butter, and swirl the pan until the sauce appears creamy. Spoon the sauce over the chicken.

VARIATIONS

• Swap in 1 pound of apples—such as Cortlands, Empires, or Northern Spy—for the pears.

• Make this with 4 boneless pork loin chops (about ¾ inch thick) in place of the chicken.

Notes

SERVES 8

ROAST PORK LOIN
with Gingerbread Stuffing

**FOR AN UNUSUAL AND DELICIOUS STUFFING FOR A BONE-IN PORK LOIN
ROAST, GINGERBREAD IS PAIRED WITH SAUTÉED ONIONS, APPLES, AND
GARLIC.** *As the pork cooks, the aroma fills the kitchen with holiday spice.
Keeping the meat on the bone makes for an especially juicy piece of pork. You
might want to have your butcher "French" the bones for you (clean off the meat
and fat) for an impressive presentation.*

Notes

5 -pound bone-in pork loin, hinged and
butterflied (have your butcher do this
for you)

1½ teaspoons salt

1 teaspoon rubbed sage

1 teaspoon dried rosemary, crumbled

½ teaspoon freshly ground black pepper

2 teaspoons extra-virgin olive oil

1 medium onion, finely chopped

1 apple, peeled and coarsely chopped

3 garlic cloves, minced

2½ cups crumbled Orange Gingerbread
(page 170)

1 large egg

Open the pork like a book. Season the pork with 1 teaspoon of the salt, and the
sage, rosemary, and pepper, rubbing it all over, on the inside and the outside.

Preheat the oven to 425°F.

In a small skillet, heat the oil over medium heat. Add the onion, apple, and
garlic and cook, stirring frequently, until the onion is tender, about 7 minutes.
Transfer to a bowl and add the gingerbread, tossing to combine. Add the egg
and remaining 1/2 teaspoon salt and mix again.

Pack the stuffing onto the open pork. Roll the pork up toward the bone side,
enclosing the stuffing. Tie the roast in several spots to keep it closed. Place in a
roasting pan and roast for 30 minutes.

Reduce the oven temperature to 350°F and roast for 30 to 35 minutes longer
or until an instant-read thermometer registers 145°F (the temperature will rise
as the pork sits). Tent with foil and let stand for 10 minutes before slicing.

VARIATION Make this with our Supermoist Corn Bread (page 158) instead of
gingerbread. You'll need 2½ cups crumbled.

HUNGARIAN PORK GOULASH

Notes

PAPRIKA GIVES THIS DISH BOTH ITS HUNGARIAN FLAIR AND DEPTH OF FLAVOR. *Since the garlic cooks for a long time, there's no need to slice or mince it. We love using a Dutch oven for stews and prefer cooking them in the oven because the temperature is even and, as a result, the stew requires no stirring.*

3 to 4 tablespoons vegetable oil

2 cups chopped onion (about 1 large)

3 cloves garlic, smashed and peeled

1 tablespoon sweet Hungarian paprika

¼ cup tomato paste

2½ pounds boneless pork shoulder, cut into 1½-inch chunks

¼ cup all-purpose flour

¾ teaspoon salt

¾ pound boiling potatoes, peeled and thinly sliced

Preheat the oven to 350°F.

In a 5-quart Dutch oven or heavy saucepan, heat 1 tablespoon of the oil over medium heat. Add the onion and garlic and cook, stirring frequently, until the onion is soft and golden brown, about 10 minutes. Stir in the paprika and tomato paste and cook for 1 minute. Set aside.

Meanwhile, in a large skillet, heat 2 tablespoons of the oil over medium-high heat. Working in batches, dredge the pork in the flour and cook until browned all over, about 6 minutes. (If necessary, add another tablespoon oil to the pan to keep the meat from sticking.) As you work, transfer the meat to the Dutch oven.

Add 1½ cups water and the salt to the Dutch oven and bring to a boil. Cover, place in the oven, and bake for 1¼ hours.

Stir in the potatoes, cover the pot, and return to the oven. Bake for 30 minutes, or until the potatoes and pork are tender.

VARIATION

• For a real treat, make this with rich and flavorful pork cheeks instead of pork shoulder. You'll find them at specialty butchers or Italian pork stores.

• Add 1 cup of sauerkraut to the pork when you add the potatoes.

Butter-Stewed
LIMA BEANS

FOR SOME REASON, LIMA BEANS HAVE GOTTEN A BAD RAP. *That's a shame, because lima beans are one of the great treats of the bean world, with a pleasantly starchy texture similar to that of chestnuts.*

2 pounds fresh lima bean pods

4 tablespoons (½ stick) unsalted butter

½ teaspoon fresh thyme

½ teaspoon salt

¼ cup chopped fresh parsley

With a paring knife, cut along the inner, curved side of the bean pods. Open the pods and pull out the beans. Place the beans in a medium saucepan and add cold water to cover by 1 inch. Add 2 tablespoons of the butter, the thyme, and the salt. Bring to a boil, reduce to a simmer, and cook uncovered until the beans are tender but not mushy, about 20 minutes.

Remove from the heat and swirl in the remaining 2 tablespoons butter and the parsley.

Lima Beans

We love the large Fordhook variety (known in the South as butter beans). Big lima beans and baby limas (which, by the way, are not immature lima beans, but just a smaller variety) are both absolutely delicious cooked with just a little butter and herbs.

We sometimes go overboard with our bean planting, but that's partly because our bean-trellising system is so ingenious that it actually creates extra room in our beds. We use sections of galvanized fencing called "hog panels," which we arch to form a sort of hoop for the beans to grow on. The wonderful side benefit of this is that it makes a shady area below that is just perfect for lettuces and other cool-loving plants.

Notes

LEEK AND POTATO GRATIN

THERE'S NOTHING LIKE THE FLAVOR OF A FRESHLY DUG POTATO. *In this luscious fall gratin, potatoes get the royal treatment.*

1½ pounds small white, red, or Yukon Gold potatoes, cut into ¼-inch slices

1 tablespoon unsalted butter

5 leeks, white and light green parts, halved lengthwise, cut crosswise into 1-inch lengths, and well washed (see below)

2 garlic cloves, thinly sliced

1 cup heavy cream

½ cup milk

¾ teaspoon salt

2 tablespoons chopped fresh parsley

Preheat the oven to 375°F.

In a pot of boiling salted water, parcook the potatoes for 5 minutes. Drain.

In a 10-inch cast-iron or other ovenproof skillet, heat the butter over medium heat. Add the leeks and garlic and cook, stirring occasionally, until the leeks are tender, 5 to 7 minutes. Transfer the leeks to a bowl.

In the same skillet, arrange half of the potatoes over the bottom. Pour ½ cup of the cream and ¼ cup of the milk over the top and sprinkle with ½ teaspoon of the salt. Top with the sautéed leeks and arrange the remaining potatoes on top. Pour the remaining ½ cup cream and ¼ cup milk over the potatoes and sprinkle with the remaining ¼ teaspoon salt. Bake for 45 minutes, or until the potatoes are tender, the top is golden brown, and most of the cream and milk have been absorbed. Serve sprinkled with the parsley.

How to Wash Leeks

If leeks are going to be cooked whole, then they should be quartered lengthwise, cutting them almost to the root end. Swish them in a bowl of water until clean. If the leeks are to be used cut up in a recipe, cut them first then clean: Place them in a bowl of tepid water and swirl them around. Scoop the leeks out with your fingers and repeat the process until no grit remains.

Notes

Butter-Crumbed
CAULIFLOWER

MOST PEOPLE KNOW CAULIFLOWER ONLY FROM THE SALAD BAR OR AS CRUDITÉS. *It's a surprisingly versatile vegetable (see Roasted Cauliflower and Apple Soup, page 90). It's both sweet and peppery, and cooking makes it mellow and brings its sweetness forward. Nutty-tasting brown butter plays off the mild cauliflower quite well.*

1 head cauliflower (about 2 pounds), separated into florets

4 tablespoons unsalted butter

½ teaspoon salt

⅛ teaspoon grated nutmeg

¼ cup panko bread crumbs

Place the cauliflower in a steamer basket set over (not in) about 1 inch of water in a skillet or saucepan. Cover the pot and bring to a boil. Steam until the cauliflower is just tender, 5 to 7 minutes. Remove the steamer basket with the cauliflower.

In a large skillet, melt the butter over medium heat. Add the cauliflower, salt, and nutmeg and cook, tossing frequently, until the cauliflower is lightly golden, 3 to 5 minutes. Add the panko and cook until the crumbs are golden and the butter begins to brown, about 1 minute.

How to Cut Up a Head of Cauliflower

On a cutting board, turn the cauliflower upside down so the stem end is up. Pull off the greenish leaves to expose the center stem; then, with a chef's knife or a paring knife, cut the florets off the stem. Large florets can be halved to make them smaller and more manageable.

Notes

MUSHROOM PILAF
with Pecans

A LITTLE BIT OF GARLIC, SOME SAGE, AND TOASTED PECANS MARRY WELL WITH THE EARTHY QUALITY OF THE MUSHROOMS. *In fact, the pilaf gets a double dose of mushroom flavor because the rice is cooked in mushroom broth, made with the mushroom trimmings.*

8 ounces shiitake mushrooms

8 ounces cremini mushrooms

2 garlic cloves, smashed and peeled

½ teaspoon rubbed sage

1 tablespoon extra-virgin olive oil

⅓ cup finely chopped onion or shallot

1 cup long-grain white rice

¾ teaspoon salt

1 carrot, shaved into long ribbons with a vegetable peeler

1 cup frozen peas, thawed

½ cup pecans, toasted (page 13) and broken into pieces

Preheat the oven to 350°F.

With the tip of a paring knife, cut out and remove the stems from the shiitake mushrooms. Cut up the stems and place them in a small saucepan. Thickly slice the caps. Trim off the very ends of the cremini stems and add them to the saucepan with the shiitake stems. Thickly slice the caps.

Add the garlic, sage, and 2½ cups water to the mushroom stems. Bring to a boil, reduce to a simmer, cover, and cook the mushroom broth while you sauté the onion and mushrooms.

In a medium, ovenproof saucepan, heat the oil over medium-low heat. Add the onion and cook, stirring frequently, until tender, about 5 minutes. Add the mushroom caps and stir to combine. Cook, stirring frequently, until they start to wilt, about 4 minutes.

Strain the mushroom broth into a 2-cup measure. If you don't have 2 cups, add water. Stir the rice into the saucepan with the mushrooms. Add the mushroom broth and salt and bring to a boil.

Cover, place in the oven, and bake for 20 minutes, or until the rice is tender. Uncover and, with a fork (so you don't crush the grains of rice), stir in the carrot, peas, and pecans. Cover and let sit for 5 minutes before serving.

Notes

ROASTED BEET TANGLE

BEETS WITH THEIR TOPS ON ARE WHAT WE CALL A TWO-FOR-ONE VEGETABLE. *Here, the beets are roasted and the greens are sautéed.*

2 bunches beets with greens attached (about 3 pounds total)

3 tablespoons olive oil

2 garlic cloves, thinly sliced

1 sprig fresh rosemary (about 3 inches long)

1 tablespoon brown mustard

1 tablespoon red wine vinegar

½ teaspoon salt

Preheat the oven to 425°F. Cut off the tops of the beets right where they meet the beets and set aside.

Rinse the beets and wrap in foil (if they are of a similar size, you can wrap several together). Place on a baking sheet and bake 1 to 1¼ hours (depending upon their size and age), or until the beets yield to gentle pressure. When they're cool enough to handle, unwrap the beets and slip the skins off (use a paper towel or a pair of kitchen gloves so you don't stain your hands). Cut the beets into thick wedges.

Meanwhile, working with one green at a time, hold a beet green by its stem and, with the other hand, push the green off the stem and discard the stem; don't worry if some of the stem stays attached. Place the greens in a bowl and wash them in several changes of water until the water is clear and there's no grit clinging to the beet greens.

In a large skillet, heat 2 tablespoons of the oil over low heat. Add the garlic and rosemary and cook until the garlic begins to turn golden brown, about 4 minutes. Discard the rosemary. Add the greens to the skillet, working in batches, adding more greens to the skillet as those in the skillet wilt. Cook until the greens are tender, about 5 minutes. Transfer the greens to a large serving bowl and add the beets.

Add the mustard, vinegar, and remaining 1 tablespoon oil to the skillet and cook for about 30 seconds just to heat. Drizzle over the beets and greens, sprinkle with the salt, and toss to combine.

Notes

BRAISED FENNEL
with Pernod

PERNOD, A FRENCH APERITIF MADE WITH ANISE SEED AND LICORICE, MIMICS THE ANISE FLAVORS OF FENNEL (WHICH IS SOMETIMES LABELED ANISE IN THE MARKET). *When you trim the woody stalks off the fennel bulb, be sure to keep the fronds, the feathery-looking tops, to use in the dish.*

2 fennel bulbs (about ¾ pound each)	¼ cup Pernod
1 tablespoon olive oil	½ teaspoon salt
3 garlic cloves, smashed and peeled	¼ teaspoon freshly ground black pepper

Cut off the fennel stalks. Remove the fennel fronds from the stalks and chop to get ¼ cup. Discard the stalks. Cut the fennel bulb in half lengthwise and then thinly slice crosswise.

In a large skillet, heat the oil over medium-low heat. Add the garlic and cook until tender, 4 to 5 minutes. Add the fennel and cook, tossing frequently, until the fennel is golden brown, about 10 minutes.

Add the Pernod, salt, and pepper and cook for 1 minute. Add ¼ cup water, cover the skillet, and cook until the fennel is tender, 5 to 7 minutes. Add the fronds and toss to combine.

Fennel

Looking a little bit like celery, but with a bulbous bottom, fennel has tall green stalks and feathery fronds (which look like dill). Its texture too is much like celery's, but it has a distinctly licorice-like taste. Delicious raw (see Roasted Beet and Goat Cheese Salad, page 92), when cooked (as in Braised Fennel with Pernod, above) it becomes soft and creamy.

Notes

PUMPKIN CHEESE BREAD

IF THERE WERE EVER A SNACK HEARTY ENOUGH TO STAND UP TO A HEARTY STOUT, THIS IS IT. *A beautiful deep orange from both the pumpkin and the Cheddar, this savory loaf has autumn written all over it.*

3½ to 3¾ cups all-purpose flour, spooned and leveled (page 165)

1 tablespoon light brown sugar

2¼ teaspoons (1 envelope) rapid-rise yeast

1¼ teaspoons salt

⅛ teaspoon cayenne pepper

¾ cup canned unsweetened pumpkin puree (not pumpkin pie mix)

1 cup (4 ounces) shredded medium or sharp yellow Cheddar cheese

1 tablespoon unsalted butter, softened

1 large egg yolk, lightly beaten with 1 teaspoon water

In a large bowl, stir together 3½ cups of the flour, and the brown sugar, yeast, salt, and cayenne. Add 1 cup water, the pumpkin, and cheese, and mix until well combined. The dough will be slightly sticky.

Turn the dough out onto a lightly floured work surface and knead until it forms a smooth ball. (Add up to ¼ cup more flour if needed.) Sprinkle a large bowl with flour and add the ball of dough, turning to coat. Cover with plastic wrap and refrigerate overnight.

The next day take the dough out of the refrigerator, transfer to a lightly floured work surface, and flatten the dough to a rough rectangle with your hands. Use the butter to coat a 9 x 5-inch loaf pan. Roll the dough up into a cylindrical shape and place seam-side down in the loaf pan. Cover loosely with plastic wrap or a clean kitchen towel and let rise at room temperature for 1 to 1¼ hours, or until almost doubled in volume.

Meanwhile, when the dough has risen for 35 minutes, preheat the oven to 375°F.

Slash the loaf down the center with a sharp knife. Brush the loaf with the egg-water wash. Bake for 50 minutes, or until the bottom of the loaf sounds hollow when tapped. Turn the bread out of the pan and onto a rack. Serve warm or at room temperature.

CINNAMON-GINGER APPLESAUCE

HOMEMADE APPLESAUCE IS A SNAP TO MAKE, AND IF YOU USE AN ASSORTMENT OF APPLES, ALL WITH DIFFERENT FLAVOR PROFILES, IT MAKES A MORE INTERESTING SAUCE. *You don't have to bother to peel or seed the apples, because once they are cooked they are put through a food mill. Cooking the apples with the skins on gives the applesauce a pink blush. (Of course if you don't have a food mill, then peel and seed the apples first.) Applesauce freezes well, so if you don't plan on using it within a few days, portion it out and freeze. It should last about 6 months.*

¼ cup sugar, plus more to taste

1 cinnamon stick, split lengthwise, or ½ teaspoon ground

¼ cup thinly sliced fresh ginger

1 vanilla bean, split lengthwise, or ½ teaspoon pure vanilla extract

Pinch of salt

3 pounds assorted apples, cut into eighths

In a large saucepan, stir together ¼ cup sugar, the cinnamon, ginger, vanilla bean (if using vanilla extract, add it later), salt, and ½ cup water. Add the apples and bring the mixture to a boil. Reduce to a simmer, cover, and cook, stirring occasionally, until the apples are tender, about 30 minutes.

Transfer the mixture to a food mill fitted with the disc with the smallest holes, and puree. Discard the skins and seeds. Taste the applesauce, and if it needs more sugar, stir it in while the applesauce is still warm. Serve warm or chilled.

VARIATION Swap in a mix of ripe Bartlett and d'Anjou pears; or, if you can find them, Packham and Comice. (Don't use Bosc, as their cooking time will be substantially different from that of the other pears.) Use light brown sugar instead of granulated sugar. Since pears are juicier than apples, start with just ¼ cup of water, adding more only if the pan seems too dry.

RUSTIC APPLE PIE

WE LOVE WHAT ROSEMARY DOES IN THIS SIMPLE PIE. *Slightly woodsy, slightly savory, and not at all what you might expect from an apple pie. Just perfect with a small scoop of vanilla ice cream.*

Basic Pie Dough (page 27)

3 tablespoons all-purpose flour

3 tablespoons sugar

1½ teaspoons chopped fresh rosemary

¼ teaspoon salt

1 pound sweet apples, such as Cortland, Northern Spy, Empire, Golden Delicious, or a combo

2 tablespoons bourbon, brandy, applejack, or dark rum

2 tablespoons unsalted butter, cut into bits

1 large egg beaten with 1 teaspoon water

On a lightly floured work surface, roll the dough out to a 12-inch round and transfer to a large baking sheet.

In a small bowl, whisk together the flour, sugar, rosemary, and salt. Sprinkle half of the mixture over the dough, leaving a 2-inch border all around.

Preheat the oven to 350°F.

Peel, core, and cut the apples into ¼-inch-thick slices. As you work, transfer the apples to a bowl and toss with the bourbon. Arrange the apples in slightly overlapping concentric circles on top of the flour mixture, leaving the same 2-inch border. (If any bourbon remains in the bowl, drizzle it over the apples.) Sprinkle the top of the apples with the remaining flour mixture. Fold the border of the pie over the apples. Dot the apple with the butter, and brush the dough with the egg wash.

Bake for 1 hour, or until the crust is golden brown and the apples are tender. Let cool on the baking sheet on a rack.

Notes

APPLE BUTTER TURNOVERS

Notes

_____
_____
_____
_____
_____
_____
_____
_____
_____
_____
_____
_____
_____
_____
_____
_____
_____
_____
_____
_____
_____
_____
_____
_____
_____
_____
_____
_____

YOU CAN HAVE DESSERT ON THE TABLE IN NO TIME WITH PUFF PASTRY IN THE FREEZER AND APPLE BUTTER ON HAND. *There isn't any butter in apple butter; it's just superconcentrated applesauce, thick and sweet.*

1 sheet frozen puff pastry (half of a 17.3 ounce package), thawed

1 tablespoon unsalted butter, melted

1 tablespoon plus 2 teaspoons sugar

¼ teaspoon ground cinnamon

⅛ teaspoon ground cardamom

⅛ teaspoon ground ginger

Pinch of salt

¾ cup apple butter, homemade (see below), or store-bought

1 large egg, beaten

Preheat the oven to 400°F. Line a baking sheet with parchment paper.

On a lightly floured work surface, roll the puff pastry out to a 10-inch square. Cut the pastry into four 5-inch squares.

Brush the squares on one side with the melted butter. In a small bowl, combine 1 tablespoon of the sugar with the cinnamon, cardamom, ginger, and salt. Sprinkle over the butter.

Spoon 3 tablespoons of apple butter onto the bottom half of each square, leaving a ¾-inch border on the bottom and 2 sides. Brush the border with the beaten egg and fold the top over to enclose the filling. Transfer the turnovers to the baking sheet. Brush the tops of the turnovers with the beaten egg and sprinkle with the remaining 2 teaspoons sugar. With a paring knife or a pair of scissors, make 2 small steam vents in the turnovers. Bake for 20 minutes, or until puffed and golden brown.

Apple Butter

You can make your own apple butter by making the Cinnamon-Ginger Applesauce on page 118 and cooking it down, very slowly, on top of the stove until it's thick enough for a spoon to stand up in it.

CARAMELIZED PEAR BREAD PUDDING

BREAD PUDDINGS, FOR THE MOST PART, ARE HOMEY, BUT THIS ONE IS A BIT MORE SOPHISTICATED. *A little bit of lemon juice added to the sugar prevents the sugar from crystallizing as it caramelizes. We use Bosc pears because they hold up well and don't fall apart as they cook.*

½ cup plus 3 tablespoons sugar

1 tablespoon fresh lemon juice

¼ teaspoon salt

1½ pounds firm-ripe Bosc pears (about 4), peeled, halved lengthwise, and thinly sliced crosswise

2 tablespoons unsalted butter

¼ teaspoon grated nutmeg

¼ teaspoon ground ginger

¼ teaspoon ground cinnamon

3 large eggs

3 large egg yolks

2 tablespoons brandy

3 cups half-and-half

12 slices (½ inch thick) Italian bread, toasted

In a large skillet, combine 3 tablespoons of the sugar, the lemon juice, and the salt. Cook over medium heat until the sugar has melted and starts to color slightly, about 3 minutes. Add the pears and butter and cook, stirring frequently, until tender but not mushy, about 10 minutes (timing may vary).

In a large bowl, whisk together the remaining ½ cup sugar, the nutmeg, ginger, cinnamon, whole eggs, egg yolks, and brandy. Whisk in the half-and-half.

Place 6 of the slices of bread in a 9-inch square baking dish. Top with the pears, then the remaining slices of bread, pressing the bread down on the pears. Pour the half-and-half mixture over all. Let stand for 30 minutes at room temperature, occasionally pressing on the top layer of bread to submerge it.

Preheat the oven to 325°F.

Line the bottom of a large baking dish (large enough to hold the baking dish with the pears) with newspaper, paper towels, or a kitchen cloth for insulation so the bottom doesn't overcook or separate. Place the baking dish in the larger baking dish. Place the larger baking dish on a pulled-out oven rack and pour hot water to come halfway up the sides of the smaller baking dish. Bake for 1 hour, or until the custard is set. Remove from the water bath. Serve warm or chilled.

Notes

Company's Coming

APPLE CAKE

THIS IS THE PERFECT CAKE TO HAVE ON HAND FOR EITHER EXPECTED OR UNEXPECTED COMPANY. *It'll make a hefty amount and will keep for several days at room temperature. Sandy's mother-in-law, Margaret Stieber, grew up on a farm in Sheboygan, Wisconsin, and this was the cake she and her mom baked for the farm hands (thirty of them) that came to help with the threshing of the wheat. You can use any type of apple here, with the following exceptions: Granny Smiths tend to be too dry and McIntoshes break down too much and get mushy.*

⁍[CAKE]⁌

2 sticks (8 ounces) unsalted butter, softened

1 cup granulated sugar

½ cup packed dark brown sugar

2½ cups all-purpose flour, spooned and leveled (page 165)

2 teaspoons ground cinnamon

1 teaspoon baking powder

1 teaspoon baking soda

¾ teaspoon salt

2 large eggs

1 cup buttermilk

2 cups diced (½ inch) peeled apple (from 2 to 3 apples)

⁍[NUT CRUNCH TOPPING]⁌

½ cup granulated sugar

3 tablespoons all-purpose flour

1½ teaspoons ground cinnamon

3 tablespoons cold unsalted butter, cut into bits

¾ cup coarsely chopped pecans or walnuts

FOR THE CAKE Preheat the oven to 350°F. Grease a 9 x 13-inch baking pan.*

With a mixer, beat the butter until creamy. Gradually beat in the granulated and brown sugars, and beat until light and fluffy. In a separate bowl, whisk together the flour, cinnamon, baking powder, baking soda, and salt.

Add the eggs to the butter mixture, one at a time, beating well after each addition. Add the flour mixture, alternating with the buttermilk, beginning and ending with the flour mixture. Fold in the apples just until combined. Scrape the mixture into the pan.

Recipe continues

Notes

Apples

Apples are New York State's largest fruit crop. The Empire apple, a cross between Red Delicious and McIntosh, was introduced in 1966, and it's a crisp, sweet-tart apple. It also happens to be the one we grow at the Beekman. It makes sensational applesauce, is wonderful in a pie (because of the cross with Red Delicious, it doesn't collapse the way a Mac does in a pie), makes a superb apple dumpling, and it is just right for eating on its own or with a hunk of cheese. We're also fond of Winesaps, Cortlands, and Northern Spys, but truth is, we've rarely met an apple we didn't like.

FOR THE TOPPING With a pastry blender or two knives used scissors fashion, cut together the sugar, flour, cinnamon, and butter until the mixture resembles fat, coarse crumbs. Stir in the nuts. Scatter the topping over the cake batter in an even layer.

Bake for 50 minutes, or until a toothpick inserted in the center comes out with just a few moist crumbs attached. Cool in the pan on a rack. Serve directly from the pan.

*The cake is served from the pan, but if you would like to transfer it to a serving platter instead, do this: Before baking, grease the pan and then line the pan with a layer of heavy-duty foil or a double layer of regular foil, leaving a 2-inch overhang at the short ends. Butter the foil. Once the cake is done and cooled, lift it out of the pan using the overhang as handles.

Homemade "Buttermilk"

If you need buttermilk for baking (as opposed to drinking) and find yourself without any, here's what you do. For every cup of buttermilk you need, place 2 tablespoons of cider vinegar or lemon juice into a 1-cup glass measure and add enough milk (any kind from 1% to whole milk) to equal a cup. Let it stand at room temperature for 1 hour. Another option is to use plain yogurt and add enough water to thin to the consistency of buttermilk.

Baked Apple Dumplings

IT'S LIKE HAVING YOUR OWN INDIVIDUAL APPLE PIE. *When apples are at their peak, they need little seasoning, as they are bursting with flavor. At other times of year you might want to add a little cinnamon or other spice (mix it in with the sugar).*

Basic Pie Dough (page 27)

2 tablespoons plain dried bread crumbs

4 small sweet apples (6 to 8 ounces each)

2 tablespoons fresh lemon juice

4 teaspoons light brown sugar

4 teaspoons unsalted butter

1 large egg beaten with 1 teaspoon water

Preheat the oven to 400°F. Line a baking sheet with parchment paper.

On a lightly floured work surface, roll the dough out to a 12-inch square. Cut into four 6-inch squares. Scatter the bread crumbs in the center of each square.

Peel the apples, leaving them whole. Core the apples, going straight through to the bottom. Drizzle the lemon juice into the cavity and over the apples. Place the apples on top of the dough squares.

Place 1 teaspoon brown sugar and 1 teaspoon butter into each apple. Gently pull the dough up and around the apple, pinching at the top to seal. Place the apples on the baking sheet and brush the dough with the egg wash.

Bake for 20 to 25 minutes, or until the crust is golden brown. Let cool for 10 minutes before serving.

VARIATION Stuff chopped walnuts, pecans, golden raisins, dried cranberries, or small cubes of caramel into the center of each apple for an even more decadent dessert.

Notes

*Winter must
be cold for those
with no warm
memories.*

—ALFRED HAYES

WINTER

When little, Brent was mesmerized by his grandmother's collection of holiday snow globes—perfect little settings surrounded by whirling, glittery snow. These unobtainable, glass-bound worlds were made all the more foreign by the southern (snowless) climes of his childhood.

The kitchen at the Beekman is surrounded by windows on three sides, and sometimes on quiet, gray winter days when the snow is swirling, it is not hard to imagine that we are sitting inside one of those tiny snow-globe houses, illuminated by an unseen fire within.

This probably explains why it takes Brent so long to fetch something from the root cellar for a winter's meal. Lost amid the glass canning jars, he is hypnotized by their silent, suspended bounties of summer.

Continue

POACHED FIGS

with Blaak Cheese

Notes

THE ESSENTIAL INGREDIENT IN OUR BEEKMAN 1802 GENEROUS FRUITCAKE IS FIG, SO WE ALWAYS HAVE PLENTY ON HAND THIS TIME OF YEAR. *Plump, dried Calimyrna figs (a California version of the Smyrna fig from Turkey) become juicy and spicy when cooked in a sweet poaching liquid. Serve the figs along with Rosemary Spiced Nuts (page 132).*

½ cup packed light brown sugar

1 vanilla bean, split lengthwise, seeds scraped into pan

1 cinnamon stick

½ teaspoon coriander seeds

8 whole cloves

1 bay leaf

¼ teaspoon freshly ground black pepper

⅛ teaspoon salt

6 strips lime zest

1 tablespoon fresh lime juice

1 pound dried Calimyrna figs

1 pound Blaak cheese

In a medium saucepan, combine 2 cups water, the brown sugar, vanilla bean, cinnamon stick, coriander seeds, cloves, bay leaf, pepper, salt, lime zest, and lime juice. Bring to a simmer over medium heat and cook for 5 minutes.

Add the figs, cover, and simmer until tender, 30 to 40 minutes. Let the figs cool in the liquid. Arrange the figs on a platter with the chunk of cheese.

Blaak Cheese

Beekman 1802 Blaak is the first artisanal cheese produced from the goats at Beekman Farm. Blaak is an Italian-style semihard cheese made from a mix of unpasteurized goat and cow milk, which gives the cheese a mild but distinctive flavor. This rare cheese is aged for 4 months in our caves and is coated with ash at each turning to promote the ripening of the wheel. The resulting edible black rind gives the cheese its name. Blaak has the texture of a young Parmesan or Spanish manchego, but with a tangier, earthier flavor. Good substitutes would be Parmesan, manchego, or goat Gouda.

ROSEMARY SPICED NUTS

THE PERFECT MARRIAGE OF WOODSY ROSEMARY, SMOKY ANCHO CHILE POWDER, AND RICH NUTS. *We like this particular combination of nuts, but feel free to use your favorites.*

1 cup pecans

1 cup roasted cashews

1 cup natural (unblanched) almonds

1 tablespoon sugar

1 tablespoon chopped fresh rosemary

1½ teaspoons ancho chile powder

1 teaspoon salt

3 tablespoons unsalted butter, melted

Preheat the oven to 350°F.

Place the pecans, cashews, and almonds on a rimmed baking sheet. In a small bowl, mix together the sugar, rosemary, chile powder, and salt.

Pour the melted butter over the nuts, tossing to coat. Sprinkle the sugar mixture over the nuts and toss again. Bake for 10 to 12 minutes, tossing once, until the nuts are crisp and lightly browned. Let cool to room temperature. Store in an airtight container for up to 2 weeks.

Notes

ROASTED RED PEPPER AND ALMOND CROSTINI

MAKES 40 CROSTINI

INSPIRED BY A SPANISH ROMESCO SAUCE, THE SLIGHTLY SMOKY, PLEASANTLY HOT SPREAD FOR THESE CROSTINI IS RICH WITH GARLIC-SAUTÉED ALMONDS AND ROASTED RED PEPPER PUREE.

1 baguette, thinly sliced

4 tablespoons extra-virgin olive oil

2 red bell peppers

3 garlic cloves, smashed and peeled

¾ cup natural (unblanched) almonds

2 tablespoons tomato paste

¾ teaspoon paprika

¾ teaspoon salt

⅛ teaspoon cayenne pepper

Preheat the oven to 350°F.

Place the baguette slices on a large baking sheet and brush with 2 tablespoons of the oil. Bake for 5 to 7 minutes, or until the bread is golden brown. Cool on a rack.

Turn the oven to broil. With the peppers standing stem end up, cut off four flat lengthwise panels from each pepper. Place the pepper panels skin side up on a broiler pan and broil 4 inches from the heat for 10 minutes, or until the skin is charred. Transfer the peppers to a bowl and, when they're cool enough to handle, peel them.

Meanwhile, in a small skillet, heat the remaining 2 tablespoons oil over low heat. Add the garlic and cook until beginning to color slightly, 3 to 5 minutes. Add the almonds and cook until they begin to darken, about 3 minutes. Transfer the mixture to a food processor.

Add the roasted peppers, tomato paste, paprika, salt, and cayenne and pulse until still slightly chunky. Spread the mixture on the crostini to serve.

VARIATIONS

• Use the roasted red pepper spread as a pasta sauce: Cook 8 ounces of pasta and toss with the red pepper spread and a splash of cream.

• Stuff 1 tablespoon of the red pepper spread under the skin of chicken breasts before roasting or baking.

Notes

SPICED TEA

Notes

FORGET ABOUT HOT CHOCOLATE. *This is what fills our thermos when hunting down the perfect Christmas tree. The spice infusion has a complexity of flavor: a hint of citrus (coriander), licorice (anise), and sweet spices (allspice, cinnamon). Cardamom adds an air of mystery with its faintly perfumed aroma.*

SPICE INFUSION

1¼ teaspoons coriander seeds

1¼ teaspoons allspice berries

1 cinnamon stick, split lengthwise

6 whole cloves

1 teaspoon green cardamom pods, cracked

¾ teaspoon anise seed

3 strips orange zest (about 3 x ½ inch)

3 tablespoons sugar

SPICED TEA (1 SERVING)

½ cup boiling water

½ teaspoon loose black tea leaves

½ cup Spice Infusion

FOR THE SPICE INFUSION In a medium saucepan, combine the spices, orange zest, sugar, and 3 cups water and bring to a boil. Reduce to a simmer, partially cover, and cook for 20 minutes. Remove from the heat, cover, and let stand until cooled to room temperature, about 20 minutes. Strain. (The spice infusion will keep in the refrigerator for up to 3 weeks.)

FOR THE TEA For one serving, pour the just-boiled water into a mug with the loose tea. Let stand for 4 minutes. Strain and stir in the spice infusion.

VARIATIONS

• You can play around with the spices and flavorings here. Not a fan of anise? Omit the anise and increase the coriander seeds to 2 teaspoons.

• If you like ginger, add 5 thin slices to the ingredients when simmering.

• For a different sweet taste, try swapping in dark brown sugar or maple syrup for the granulated sugar.

• For a milky drink, like a chai tea, add 2 tablespoons heated whole milk to each cup of tea.

EGGNOG

THINK OF A SUPERRICH FRENCH VANILLA ICE CREAM ... *now imagine it melted and you've got this terrific glass of eggnog. If the kids are imbibing, don't add the bourbon to the eggnog and let the adults pour a little bourbon into their own glasses. Caroling is sure to follow.*

3 cups half-and-half

⅔ cup sugar

3 large eggs

3 large egg yolks

½ teaspoon grated nutmeg

3 tablespoons bourbon (optional)

In a large, heavy-bottomed saucepan, bring 2½ cups of the half-and-half to a simmer over medium heat. Have a strainer set over a bowl ready for straining the eggnog.

Meanwhile, in a medium bowl, whisk together the sugar, whole eggs, and egg yolks until light and pale. Gradually whisk the hot cream into the egg mixture; then whisk the mixture back into the saucepan and cook over low heat, whisking constantly, until the mixture is thick enough to coat the back of a spoon and registers 140°F on an instant-read thermometer. Remove from the heat and immediately strain into the bowl. Stir in the nutmeg and the remaining ½ cup half-and-half.

Let cool to room temperature. Add the bourbon (if using) and refrigerate to chill. Serve chilled.

VARIATION If you've got an ice cream machine, use it to turn the eggnog into eggnog ice cream.

Notes

MACARONI AND CHEESE

with Mushrooms and Kale

Notes

GOOD OLD MAC AND CHEESE, BUT WITH A SOPHISTICATED EDGE. *Smoked paprika, mushrooms (porcini and cremini), and kale add great flavor.*

¾ pound kale, stems cut from leaves (about 5½ cups)

8 ounces elbow macaroni

½ ounce (½ cup) dried porcini, rinsed

3 tablespoons olive oil

4 garlic cloves, minced

¾ pound cremini mushrooms, halved and thinly sliced

¼ teaspoon dried thyme

¼ teaspoon rubbed sage

¼ cup all-purpose flour

2 cups milk

1½ teaspoons sweet smoked paprika

1 teaspoon salt

2½ cups (10 ounces) shredded sharp Cheddar cheese

2 tablespoons unsalted butter

½ cup panko bread crumbs

In a large pot of boiling salted water, cook the kale for 5 minutes. With a slotted spoon, transfer the kale to a colander (keep the pot of cooking water at a boil). Run the kale under cold water to stop the cooking and then drain and squeeze out any liquid. Coarsely chop.

Add the macaroni to the boiling kale-cooking water and cook according to package directions. Drain.

Meanwhile, in a small bowl, combine the dried porcini with 1 cup warm water. Let stand until the mushrooms have softened, about 20 minutes. With your fingers, lift the mushrooms from their soaking liquid, leaving the grit behind. Line a fine-mesh sieve with paper towels, a paper coffee filter, or cheesecloth. Pour the mushroom-soaking liquid through the sieve into a bowl. Reserve the liquid. Coarsely chop the mushrooms.

Preheat the oven to 350°F.

In a 5-quart Dutch oven or other large, heavy-bottomed pot, heat the oil over medium heat. Add the garlic and cook, stirring frequently, until tender, about 2 minutes. Add the porcini and cremini mushrooms, thyme, and sage and cook, stirring occasionally, until the mushrooms have wilted and released their juices, about 5 minutes. *Recipe continues*

Cooking Greens

Swiss chard, kale, mustard greens, as well as the tops of beets and turnips, are all treated in a similar fashion. Start by cleaning thoroughly in several changes of water to remove the grit. The cooking method is up to you. The sturdier greens (such as collards) can be cooked for a long time in a liquid to make them tender, or you can blanch them first in boiling water and then cook them for a short period of time (see Quick Braised Collards with Pot Liquor, page 156). The more tender greens (such as Swiss chard or beet greens) can be sautéed quickly without being blanched first.

Any of the so-called cooking greens seem to like a little garlic and perhaps a touch of hot pepper, and some people sprinkle just a touch of sugar over the greens as they cook. However you cook them, be sure to serve your greens with a little bit of their cooking juices; this is what is called pot liquor, and it has lots of flavor.

Stir in the flour and cook for 2 minutes. Add the mushroom-soaking liquid, milk, paprika, and salt and cook, stirring occasionally, until the mixture has thickened, about 5 minutes. Remove from the heat and stir in the cheese until melted. Add the macaroni and kale and toss to coat.

Transfer the mixture to a 9 x 13-inch glass baking dish or individual ramekins.

In a small skillet, melt the butter over medium heat. Add the panko and toss to coat. Scatter the butter crumbs over the mac and cheese. Bake for 30 minutes, or until the sauce is bubbling and the top is crunchy and golden brown.

VARIATIONS

- Swap in another green for the kale, such as escarole, or even cooked chopped broccoli.
- Use Gruyère instead of Cheddar. For an extra kick, add $1/8$ teaspoon cayenne pepper and 1 teaspoon Dijon mustard to the white sauce. Instead of buttered bread crumbs, top the casserole with crushed potato chips.
- Instead of making a large mac and cheese, separate the mixture into two 9 x 9-inch pans and freeze one, unbaked and well wrapped, for a later date. You can bake the frozen mac and cheese straight from the freezer; it should take about 45 minutes.

Chicken 'n' Dumplings

CHICKEN 'N' DUMPLINGS IS TRADITIONALLY MADE BY STEWING A WHOLE CHICKEN AND THEN PULLING THE MEAT OFF THE BONE. *We've made it simpler by using chicken thighs to make the dish both faster (no need to pull meat off the bone) and more deeply flavored (the dark meat is the most flavorful part of the chicken).*

·◦[CHICKEN]◦·

2 tablespoons vegetable oil

8 boneless, skinless chicken thighs (about 4 ounces each)

¼ cup all-purpose flour

1 large onion, coarsely chopped

2 carrots, thinly sliced

3 garlic cloves, thinly sliced

2 cups Chicken Stock (page 17) or reduced-sodium canned broth

¾ teaspoon salt

½ teaspoon dried rosemary, crumbled

1 bay leaf

·◦[DUMPLINGS]◦·

1 cup all-purpose flour

½ teaspoon salt

⅔ cup cold water

FOR THE CHICKEN In a 5-quart Dutch oven, heat the oil over medium heat. Dredge the chicken in the flour, shaking off the excess, and cook until golden brown, 2 to 3 minutes a side. Transfer to a plate.

Add the onion, carrots, and garlic to the pan and cook, stirring frequently, until the vegetables are tender, about 15 minutes. Add the stock, salt, rosemary, and bay leaf and bring to a boil. Return the chicken to the pot along with any juices from the plate. Cover and simmer until the chicken is cooked through, about 25 minutes.

MEANWHILE, FOR THE DUMPLINGS In a medium bowl, combine the flour and salt. Add the water and mix until smooth. Transfer to a lightly floured work surface and roll the dough out to a ¼-inch thickness. Cut into 2 x 1-inch rectangles. Drop the dumplings onto the simmering stew, cover, and cook until the dumplings bob to the surface, about 5 minutes.

Notes

Pasta with Cabbage, Bacon, and Chestnuts

SERVES 4

A WARMING DISH FOR A COLD WINTER'S DAY: COMFORTING EGG NOODLES TOSSED WITH EARTHY CHESTNUTS, RICH BACON, AND CABBAGE SPARKED WITH APPLE AND DILL. *You can get dry-packed roasted and peeled chestnuts in jars, especially around the winter holidays. They're usually found near the canned vegetables in the supermarket.*

1 tablespoon extra-virgin olive oil

10 ounces slab bacon, cut into ½-inch dice

1 large onion, coarsely chopped

2 garlic cloves, thinly sliced

5 cups coarsely chopped cabbage (about 10 ounces)

¾ cup Chicken Stock (page 17) or reduced-sodium canned broth

2 tablespoons cider vinegar

1 cup dry-packed roasted and peeled chestnuts

1 teaspoon salt

½ teaspoon crumbled dried rosemary

¼ teaspoon freshly ground black pepper

8 ounces wide egg noodles

½ cup chopped fresh dill

1 red apple, unpeeled, cut into ½-inch chunks

In a large skillet, heat the oil over medium heat. Add the bacon and cook until crisp and browned, about 15 minutes. With a slotted spoon, transfer the bacon to paper towels to drain.

Add the onion and garlic to the bacon fat in the skillet and cook, stirring frequently, until the onion is golden brown and tender, about 12 minutes. Add the cabbage, cover, and cook, stirring occasionally, until wilted, about 10 minutes. Uncover and add the stock, vinegar, chestnuts, salt, rosemary, and pepper. Cook until the cabbage is very tender, about 10 minutes.

Meanwhile, in a large pot of boiling salted water, cook the noodles according to package directions. Drain and return to the pot. Add the bacon, cabbage mixture, dill, and apple to the noodles, and toss to combine.

Notes

PORK ROAST

with Root Vegetables

PORK, ROOT VEGETABLES, AND A LITTLE PEAR CIDER ARE PERFECT FOR A CHILLY NIGHT. *If there are any leftover vegetables, we mash them for a breakfast hash the following morning.*

4-pound boneless pork loin, preferably shoulder end

2 garlic cloves

1 teaspoon salt

2 bay leaves, crumbled

1 teaspoon rubbed sage

½ teaspoon freshly ground black pepper

3 tablespoons extra-virgin olive oil

½ pound carrots, cut into 2-inch lengths

½ pound parsnips, halved lengthwise if large, cut into 2-inch lengths

½ pound white (purple-top) turnips, cut into 1-inch wedges

¾ pound small white potatoes, halved

½ cup pear cider

Preheat the oven to 425°F. Place the pork in a roasting pan large enough to hold it and the vegetables.

On a work surface, smash the garlic with the flat side of a knife and peel. Sprinkle the garlic with the salt and finely chop; then use the flat side of the knife to mash it to a paste. Transfer the garlic paste to a small bowl and combine with the bay leaves, sage, and pepper. Add the oil to make a paste. Rub the paste all over the pork.

Scatter the vegetables around the pork. Roast for 25 minutes.

Reduce the oven temperature to 300°F and add the cider to the pan. Tent the pork loosely with foil (leaving the vegetables uncovered) and roast for 30 minutes longer, or until the vegetables are tender and the pork registers 145°F on an instant-read thermometer. Let the pork rest for 10 minutes before slicing. Serve with the vegetables alongside and drizzled with pan juices.

ROAST CHICKEN
with Potatoes and Rosemary

PINEY, WOODSY ROSEMARY AND TART, FRESH LEMON ARE PERFECT COMPLEMENTS TO THE MEATINESS OF FARM-FRESH CHICKEN. *We rub the chicken with coarse salt before roasting to help make the skin crispy, but if you've got the time, you can salt the chicken up to 2 days ahead for an even crispier skin.*

1 whole chicken (3 to 3 ½ pounds)

Coarse salt

6 sprigs fresh rosemary

1 lemon

1 pound small potatoes, cut into ½-inch chunks

5 garlic cloves, skin on

Preheat the oven to 425°F. Place a large (at least 11-inch) cast-iron skillet or a large gratin dish in the oven to heat up for at least 10 minutes.

Meanwhile, pull out and reserve the chicken giblets for another use. Sprinkle the cavity and the skin of the chicken with coarse salt. Carefully slide your fingers under the skin of the chicken breasts and season the breasts and thighs with coarse salt. Place 4 sprigs of rosemary under the skin. Prick the lemon in several places with a fork and place it in the cavity of the chicken. Place the remaining 2 sprigs of rosemary in the cavity.

Place the chicken in the hot pan, breast side up, and roast for 25 minutes. Scatter the potatoes and garlic around the chicken, and roast for 25 to 30 minutes longer, or until the chicken is cooked through and the potatoes are golden brown and tender.

Notes

WINTER VEGETABLE SOUP

IN THE MIDDLE OF WINTER, ROOT VEGETABLES CAN BE USED TO MAKE THIS HEARTY VEGETABLE SOUP. *We've been known to spend a winter afternoon pouring boiling water over our raised beds trying to pry parsnips out of the frozen ground. In this recipe, the rutabagas are an especially nice note, adding a lovely earthy sweetness. Also called swedes, rutabagas are large, orange-fleshed turnips that are sold with a coating of wax to lengthen their shelf life.*

2 tablespoons extra-virgin olive oil

1 medium onion, coarsely chopped

3 cloves garlic, thinly sliced

4 teaspoons finely chopped fresh ginger

2 carrots, halved lengthwise and thinly sliced crosswise

½ medium rutabaga (about 6 ounces), peeled, quartered lengthwise, and thinly sliced

1 medium parsnip, halved lengthwise and thinly sliced

½ pound Yukon Gold potatoes, peeled, halved lengthwise, and thinly sliced crosswise

½ pound green cabbage, cut into ½-inch-wide strips

2 tablespoons tomato paste

3½ cups Chicken Stock (page 17), or reduced-sodium canned broth

Salt

Freshly ground black pepper

2 tablespoons fresh lemon juice

1 tablespoon sugar

2 tablespoons fresh parsley leaves, for garnish

In a large saucepan, heat the oil over medium heat. Add the onion, garlic, and ginger and cook, stirring frequently, for 3 minutes. Add the carrots, rutabaga, and parsnip, and cook, stirring frequently, until the vegetables are crisp-tender, about 7 minutes.

Stir in the potatoes, cabbage, and tomato paste, stirring to coat. Add the stock and salt to taste and bring to a boil. Reduce to a simmer, cover, and cook until the vegetables are very tender, about 20 minutes. Stir in the lemon juice and sugar, and season with salt and pepper. Serve garnished with parsley leaves.

Notes

BOURBON ROAST TURKEY
with Cornbread Stuffing

Notes

WE SOMETIMES ARGUE OVER WHO GETS TO DO THE CARVING OF THIS DELICIOUS THANKSGIVING BIRD. *Keeping the turkey covered for most of its cooking time, in a pan with a fair amount of liquid, makes for a nice, juicy turkey. Uncovering and basting for the final 30 minutes ensures crisp, beautifully golden skin. Maple syrup, molasses, brown sugar, and a little Worcestershire are reminiscent of barbecue sauce. The bourbon flavor (slightly sweet with vanilla undertones) permeates the bird and makes a wonderful gravy.*

1 turkey (about 14 pounds), rinsed and patted dry, neck and giblets removed, liver discarded

¼ cup coarse salt

1 tablespoon sugar

2 teaspoons ancho chile powder

1 juice orange

1 lime

1 small onion, halved

2 bay leaves

3 garlic cloves, unpeeled

¾ cup maple syrup (preferably grade B)

2 tablespoons molasses

2 tablespoons light brown sugar

1 tablespoon Worcestershire sauce

2 cups bourbon

⅓ cup all-purpose flour

Cornbread Stuffing (page 159)

Tuck the wing tips under the turkey by bending them back and pushing them under the wings. In a small bowl, combine the salt, sugar, and chile powder. Carefully run your fingers under the breast and thigh skin of the turkey to loosen and then season with about one-third of the salt mixture. Rub the remaining mixture in the cavity of the turkey and all over the skin. With a fork, pierce the orange and lime all over. Place them in the cavity along with the onion, bay leaves, and garlic cloves. Truss the turkey.

In a small skillet, combine the maple syrup, molasses, brown sugar, and Worcestershire sauce. Bring to a simmer and cook for 5 minutes for the flavors to concentrate.

Place the turkey on a rack and the turkey neck and giblets in the roasting pan with a lid. Pour the bourbon into the pan. Pour all but ⅓ cup of the maple syrup mixture over the turkey breast. Cover the pan (if you don't have a covered roasting pan, oil a large piece of foil and cover the pan, oiled side down) and roast the turkey, without uncovering, for 1 hour 30 minutes.

Uncover the pan and brush the turkey with the reserved maple syrup mixture. Roast for 30 minutes, uncovered, until an instant-read thermometer inserted into the thigh, without touching bone, registers 165°F.

Lift the turkey from the pan and transfer to a platter or cutting board. Tent with foil and let stand for 30 minutes. Discard the neck and giblets (or reserve for turkey stock; see Making Turkey Stock, below).

Pour the juices from the roasting pan into a gravy separator or a large measuring cup and remove the fat, reserving 3 tablespoons. If there isn't enough turkey fat, add butter to make up the difference. If you don't have 4 cups of pan juices, add water to make up the difference.

Place the turkey fat in a large saucepan over low heat. Gradually whisk in the flour and cook, whisking constantly, until the flour has browned, about 5 minutes. Gradually whisk in the 4 cups of pan juices and cook, whisking constantly, until the gravy is lightly thickened, about 10 minutes. Slice the turkey and serve with the gravy and the cornbread stuffing.

Making Turkey Stock

After serving a roast turkey, don't throw out the turkey carcass: Save it to make turkey stock. Break the carcass into large pieces and transfer to a large saucepan or stockpot along with the neck and giblets. Add cold water to cover, and bring to a boil. Reduce to a simmer, add 1 large cut-up onion, 2 sliced carrots, 3 garlic cloves, a handful of parsley, and 1 tablespoon tomato paste and simmer until the stock is very flavorful, about 3 hours. Strain.

If you've only ever eaten the plumped-up grocery store version of "turkey," switching to heritage breeds like Bourbon Red and Narragansetts might surprise you in more ways than one.

First, you'll have to get used to a little less white meat. We don't find this to be a problem at all, since nearly all of the flavor is found in the dark meat of the bird. Think dark meat is greasy? That might be because you're used to eating birds artificially raised to grow abnormal amounts of "juicy" (read: watery) white meat. The diet required to balloon up the birds' breasts adversely affects the dark meat.

Second, most heritage breeds are much smaller than your average Butterball. If buying a heritage turkey from a local farmer, don't be surprised if the largest sizes don't surpass 12 to 14 pounds. The first year we raised and harvested our own turkey, we discovered that our plucked and dressed hen weighed only 5 pounds. And we had eight people coming to dinner. Good thing we had a roast in the freezer.

Lastly, taste. Believe it or not, turkeys do have flavor! At least heritage breeds do. All the way through to their bones. We found it largely a waste of time to make stock from grocery store birds, but with heritage turkeys, one turkey carcass seems to equal two chicken carcasses when it comes to flavoring stock.

TURKEY AND SPAGHETTI SQUASH STIR-FRY

WHEN WE'RE LOOKING FOR GOOD WAYS TO USE LEFTOVER TURKEY (ASIDE FROM BRENT'S MANDATORY NEXT-DAY TURKEY AND MAYO SANDWICH), WE OFTEN TURN TO A FLEXIBLE DISH LIKE A SIMPLE STIR-FRY. *Though this can be made with whatever vegetables you have on hand, we like to use spaghetti squash when we're looking for a lighter dish—a nice relief from the heavy food of the winter holidays.*

1 spaghetti squash (about 2 pounds)

2 tablespoons extra-virgin olive oil

1 medium onion, halved and thinly sliced

1 red bell pepper, cut into thin strips

4 ounces mushrooms, thinly sliced

½ cup Turkey Stock (page 147) or Chicken Stock (page 17) or reduced-sodium canned chicken broth

3 cups diced cooked turkey (about 10 ounces)

Salt

Preheat the oven to 375°F. Pierce the spaghetti squash all over with the tip of a knife. Place on a baking sheet and bake for 1 hour, or until softened and tender. Cut the squash in half lengthwise, scoop out and discard the seeds, and with a fork, scrape out the long, spaghetti-like strands into a bowl.

In a large skillet, heat the oil over medium heat. Add the onion, bell pepper, and mushrooms and cook, tossing frequently, until the vegetables are crisp-tender, about 5 minutes.

Add the stock and cook until the vegetables are tender, about 3 minutes. Add the spaghetti squash and turkey. Season with salt and cook until the squash and turkey are heated through.

VARIATION Omit the bell pepper and mushrooms and swap in 2 cups of vegetables such as broccoli, green beans, or plum tomatoes—any of these would make good substitutes.

Notes

Celery Root Puree

CELERY ROOT, ALSO CALLED CELERIAC, RESEMBLES A GIANT BUMPY BROWN TURNIP. *It has a flavor similar to that of celery (they're related but are not the same plant) but with a hint of citrus. Many cooks prepare celery root with potatoes for an interesting mash, but this combo of celery root and rice cooked in milk makes for an incredibly creamy, light-textured puree. This recipe was inspired by a dinner party thrown by our friend and collaborator Sandy Gluck, and it's a new favorite on our winter table.*

2½ cups 2% milk

2 tablespoons long-grain white rice

¾ teaspoon salt

1¼ pounds celery root (about 1 large)

In a medium saucepan, combine the milk, rice, and salt. With a paring knife, trim the celery root and remove the skin. Cut the celery root in half and thinly slice, transferring it to the saucepan as you work (this is to prevent the celery root from discoloring, which is does quickly).

Bring the mixture to a boil, reduce to a simmer, cover, and cook until the celery root can be pierced with the tip of a knife. With a slotted spoon, scoop the celery root–rice mixture into a food processor. Add as much of the milk as it takes to be able to puree the mixture to a smooth consistency similar to that of mashed potatoes. You may not need to use all the milk. Serve warm.

VARIATION It's easy to turn this puree into a soup. Cook the rice and celery root in the milk as directed. When you puree the mixture, add enough chicken broth to thin to the desired consistency. For a garnish, heat a little olive oil with some fresh sage leaves. Cook until the sage is fried and the oil is flavorful. Drizzle the sage oil over the soup, and garnish with the sage leaves and some shaved Parmesan cheese.

Notes

Maple-Glazed Candied Sweet Potatoes

THE BEEKMAN IS SURROUNDED BY MAPLE FARMS, AND NUMEROUS BOTTLES OF SYRUP ARE LEFT ON OUR DOORSTEP WHEN THE SAP IS RUNNING, EVERY SPRING AND FALL. *We put it to good use in many recipes, but nowhere is it better suited than this one. Choose a mix of sweet potatoes or simply one kind for this sweet, tart, and mildly smoky dish. These potatoes are not thickly coated with a sugary glaze, but lightly coated with maple syrup. If you can find it, seek out dark brown grade B syrup; it's deeper in flavor than grade A (amber) syrup.*

2 pounds sweet potatoes

¼ cup maple syrup (preferably grade B)

2 tablespoons unsalted butter

2 tablespoons fresh lime juice

1 teaspoon ancho chile powder

1 teaspoon salt

2 tablespoons chopped parsley, for garnish (optional)

Peel the sweet potatoes and cut into 2-inch chunks.

In a steamer basket set over (not in) boiling water, cook the potatoes until firm-tender, about 10 minutes. Remove from the basket.

In a large skillet, heat the maple syrup, butter, lime juice, chile powder, and salt over medium heat. When the syrup starts to bubble, add the sweet potatoes. Cook, tossing frequently, until the maple mixture is quite thick and the potatoes are well coated and cooked through, about 7 minutes.

If you like, garnish with parsley.

Notes

BRUSSELS SPROUTS
with Bacon and Roasted Chestnuts

NEITHER OF US WAS A FAN AS A CHILD, BUT WE'VE GROWN TO LOVE THEM. *Cooked until crisp-tender, Brussels sprouts are sweet and delicate. They are paired here with bacon and roasted chestnuts, two classic partners that add to the hearty and earthy flavors in this dish. For the deepest flavor, you should roast your own chestnuts, but for the sake of convenience you can use store-bought roasted and peeled chestnuts, which come in jars.*

1 tablespoon olive oil	½ teaspoon salt
3 slices bacon, coarsely chopped	¾ pound chestnuts, roasted
1 pound Brussels sprouts, trimmed and halved lengthwise	1 tablespoon cold unsalted butter

In a large skillet, heat the oil over medium-low heat. Add the bacon and cook, stirring occasionally, until lightly crisped, about 5 minutes. With a slotted spoon, transfer the bacon to a paper towel to drain, then crumble.

Add the Brussels sprouts to the skillet and cook, tossing frequently, until lightly browned, about 5 minutes. Add the salt and 1 cup water, cover, and simmer until the sprouts are almost tender, about 8 minutes. Check the sprouts with the tip of a paring knife; if it goes in with just the slightest bit of resistance, the sprouts are done.

Add the chestnuts and cook uncovered until the sprouts are crisp-tender, the chestnuts are piping hot, and most of the liquid has evaporated, about 3 minutes. Remove from the heat and swirl in the cold butter until creamy. Scatter the bacon over the top and serve.

VARIATION Omit the bacon and increase the oil to 2 tablespoons. Scatter ¼ cup coarsely chopped pecans or walnuts over the Brussels sprouts before serving.

GLAZED CARROTS
with Pine Nuts and Raisins

SWEET CARROTS COOKED WITH GARLIC AND HOT PEPPER ARE TOSSED WITH
GOLDEN RAISINS AND PINE NUTS—A CLASSIC SICILIAN COMBINATION.

2 tablespoons olive oil

4 garlic cloves, thinly sliced

1 teaspoon hot pepper flakes

2 pounds carrots, cut on the diagonal
    into ½-inch-thick slices

2 tablespoons sugar

1 teaspoon salt

2 tablespoons slivered lemon zest

⅓ cup golden raisins

¼ cup pine nuts, toasted

In a large saucepan, heat the oil over low heat. Add the garlic and cook until
golden brown, about 4 minutes. Add the hot pepper flakes and stir to combine.

Add the carrots, sugar, salt, and 1 cup water and bring to a boil. Reduce the
heat slightly and cook rapidly until the liquid has evaporated and the carrots
are tender and glazed, about 10 minutes.

Add the lemon zest, raisins, and pine nuts and toss to combine.

Carrots

Until people garden, they generally have no idea how many different kinds of
carrots there are. Some of our favorites are the spicy Cosmic Carrot, which
has a pretty red-purple skin and orange flesh, and the creamy Belgian White,
which was introduced sometime before 1863. Carrots have the added benefit
of being "self-storers," meaning they can be left in the garden until winter,
covered with straw. In milder winters, we've been known to pull fresh carrots
on New Year's Eve.

It's always best to clip the greens from the carrots (about an inch from
the carrot top) to keep them firmer in the refrigerator. A few greens added to
stock can add a depth of flavor that celery alone doesn't. When we have too
many carrots to eat at once, we also juice them and freeze the juice to make
garden cocktails throughout the winter (great with vodka, ginger, and lemon).

Notes

SMASHED POTATOES

Notes

SMASHED, NOT MASHED—THEY'VE GOT SOME TEXTURE. *A potato masher is the perfect tool to use here, and you can smash the potatoes right in the pan. If you aren't a fan of potato skins, you can remove them before the smashing, but they provide extra texture and fiber.*

1 pound small white boiling potatoes

½ teaspoon salt

1 tablespoon unsalted butter

1 tablespoon olive oil

⅓ cup milk

Place potatoes in a large saucepan and add cold water to cover. Bring to a boil, add some salt, and reduce the heat to a gentle, but not rolling, boil. This is so the potatoes don't burst in their skins and become waterlogged. Cook until the potatoes can easily be pierced with the tip of a knife, 20 to 30 minutes. Drain.

In a large skillet, melt the butter in the oil over medium heat. Add the drained potatoes, milk, and salt. With a potato masher, smash the potatoes in the skillet so they are still quite lumpy and the dish is piping hot.

Potatoes

Of all vegetables, potatoes are probably one of the most versatile, especially when one considers the heirloom varieties. From the purple-fleshed Purple Peruvian, to the pink-hued Huckleberry, to creamy fingerling varietals, potatoes can be a more surprising addition to the plate than what most people remember from their mom's comfort-food side dishes. One thing Mom was right about, however, was that most of their nutrition (not to mention most of their taste) is found in their skins. So whether they're baked, roasted, or mashed, we usually like to leave the skins on—well scrubbed, of course.

There's one situation in which we think you should always peel potatoes, and that is if you don't buy organic (which we think you should). If you are concerned about pesticides, be aware that potatoes usually top the list of the vegetables with the most pesticide residue.

UTICA GREENS

THOUGH IT'S A FAVORITE OF OURS, WE DIDN'T MAKE UP THE NAME OF THIS DISH. *It's named for Utica, a city in central New York State, which for some reason—perhaps having to do with its large Italian population—is known for this wonderful side vegetable. Escarole, a mild green that can be eaten raw or cooked, is served up with a crisp topping of Parmesan cheese and bread crumbs. One taste and you'll understand why we love it.*

2 bunches escarole (about 1¼ pounds total), cut into wide ribbons

1 tablespoon extra-virgin olive oil

3 cloves garlic, thinly sliced

1 small piece fresh or dried hot red chile pepper

½ teaspoon salt

½ cup grated Parmesan cheese

¼ cup panko bread crumbs

Preheat the oven to 350°F.

In a large pot of boiling salted water, cook the escarole until tender, about 5 minutes. Drain well.

In a large ovenproof skillet, heat the oil over medium-low heat. Add the garlic and chile pepper and cook until the garlic starts to get golden, about 3 minutes. Add the escarole, sprinkle with the salt, and cook, tossing, until hot, about 3 minutes.

Sprinkle the mixture with the Parmesan and panko. Place in the oven and bake for 5 to 7 minutes, or until the cheese has melted and the crumbs are browned.

Notes

SERVES 4

QUICK BRAISED COLLARDS

with Pot Liquor

LONG, SLOW COOKING IS WHAT'S USUALLY ASSOCIATED WITH COLLARD GREENS, BUT THESE COOK IN A MERE FIFTEEN MINUTES AND ARE TENDER AND SWEET. *The secret? A five-minute blanching of the greens in boiling water gives them a huge head start on softening up.*

2 bunches collard greens (about ¾ pound each)	¾ cup Chicken Stock (page 17) or reduced-sodium canned broth
1 tablespoon olive oil	1 tablespoon cider vinegar
3 garlic cloves, smashed and peeled	¼ teaspoon hot pepper flakes
½ teaspoon salt	

With a paring knife, cut the ribs out of each collard green. Stack and roll the greens up like a cigar. Then cut them crosswise into ribbons. In a large pot of boiling salted water, cook the greens for 5 minutes. Drain.

In a large skillet, heat the oil over medium-low heat. Add the garlic and cook until starting to turn golden, about 4 minutes.

Add the blanched collards to the pan, sprinkle with the salt, and add the stock. Cook, stirring occasionally, until the collards are very tender, about 10 minutes. Stir in the vinegar, sprinkle with the hot pepper flakes, and serve the collards with their pan juices.

VARIATIONS

• Add ½ pound diced smoked sausage when you sauté the collards.

• If you want the smoked flavor without the heat, add some sweet smoked paprika to the collards as they're sautéed.

• Omit the hot pepper flakes and pass hot sauce at the table so diners can season the collards themselves.

Notes

SUPERMOIST CORN BREAD

MOIST, DENSE, AND DELICIOUS ON ITS OWN OR DRIZZLED WITH HONEY, THIS IS OUR CORN BREAD OF CHOICE FOR STUFFING A TURKEY. *What we love about this corn bread is that it's not the supersweet, cakelike kind. Ours is made with stone-ground cornmeal (for extra texture) and is then baked in a hot cast-iron skillet for a crunchy crust and a moist interior. (If don't have a large cast-iron skillet, use a heavy 10-inch cake pan instead.)*

$1\frac{1}{2}$ cups coarse yellow cornmeal

2 tablespoons sugar

$\frac{3}{4}$ teaspoon baking soda

$\frac{3}{4}$ teaspoon salt

$1\frac{1}{4}$ cups buttermilk

$\frac{1}{2}$ cup sour cream

2 large eggs

1 stick (4 ounces) unsalted butter

Preheat the oven to 425°F. Place a 10-inch cast-iron skillet in the oven while you prepare the batter.

In a large bowl, whisk together the cornmeal, sugar, baking soda, and salt.

In a separate bowl or large glass measuring cup, stir together the buttermilk, sour cream, and eggs until well combined. Carefully take the hot skillet out of the oven, add the butter, and swirl to melt. Stir the melted butter into the buttermilk mixture.

Make a well in the center of the dry ingredients and dump in the buttermilk mixture. Stir until just combined; then scrape the batter into the hot skillet. Bake for 25 minutes, or until golden brown with a crusty top.

VARIATIONS

- You can make the corn bread with olive oil instead of butter. Place the oil in the skillet before it's preheated.
- With a slight modification, you can use the same batter to make corncakes: Increase the buttermilk to $1\frac{1}{2}$ cups, and increase the melted butter to 1 stick plus 1 tablespoon. Drop the batter by $\frac{1}{4}$ cupful into a greased pan or onto a griddle, and cook until crisp and golden, about 3 minutes per side.

Notes

CORN BREAD STUFFING

OUR HOMEMADE CORN BREAD MAKES FOR THE TASTIEST STUFFING. *We bake our stuffing—or perhaps we should call it dressing—outside of the turkey, but each family has its own tradition.*

Notes

Supermoist Corn bread (page 158)

1 tablespoon extra-virgin olive oil

1 large onion, coarsely chopped

1 pound sweet Italian sausage (without fennel seeds)

1 cup dry-packed roasted and peeled chestnuts

½ cup chopped fresh parsley leaves

Grated zest of 1 lemon

1½ cups Chicken Stock (page 17) or reduced-sodium canned broth

1 stick (4 ounces) unsalted butter, melted

1¼ teaspoons salt

½ teaspoon freshly ground black pepper

Bake the corn bread at least 2 days before you plan on making the stuffing. Cut the corn bread into 1-inch chunks, place on a baking sheet in a single layer, and let dry out at room temperature.

Preheat the oven to 350°F.

In a large skillet, heat the oil over medium heat. Add the onion and cook, stirring frequently, until the onion is tender, about 7 minutes. Remove the sausages from their casings and crumble into the skillet. Cook, stirring occasionally, until the sausage is cooked through, 5 to 7 minutes. Transfer the mixture to a large bowl.

Add the chestnuts, parsley, and lemon zest to the bowl along with the corn bread cubes, and toss to combine. Add the chicken stock, melted butter, salt, and pepper, and toss until moistened. The crumbs will break up, and that's fine. Transfer to a 9 x 13-inch baking dish.

Cover and bake for 20 minutes. Uncover and bake for 20 minutes longer, or until the stuffing is piping hot and crusty on the top.

VARIATION Sauté a stalk or two of diced celery along with the onion. Swap in toasted pecans for the chestnuts and add a handful of dried cherries to the mixture.

CRANBERRY AND DRIED CHERRY SAUCE

SOME PEOPLE WOULDN'T CONSIDER THE HOLIDAY TABLE COMPLETE WITHOUT CRANBERRY SAUCE, AND EVERYONE SEEMS TO HAVE A FAVORITE. *This one is sweet from the sugar, cherries, and orange juice, balanced by a slightly bitter note from the orange skin. Use our recipe as a starting point for creating your own family's tradition.*

1 package (12 ounces) fresh cranberries

⅔ cup sugar

½ navel orange, cut into ½-inch bits

½ cup dried cherries

¼ teaspoon salt

In a medium, heavy-bottomed saucepan, combine the cranberries, sugar, orange, cherries, and salt. Cook over medium-low heat, stirring frequently, until most of the berries have popped and the sauce is thick, about 10 minutes. Let cool to room temperature; then refrigerate. (The sauce will keep refrigerated for 2 weeks.)

Notes

Spiced Carrot Cake

ADDING ROASTED CASHEWS AND INDIAN SPICES TO A CARROT CAKE LIFTS THIS AMERICAN CLASSIC WAY OUT OF THE ORDINARY. *And what would a carrot cake be without a cream cheese frosting? (Not a carrot cake!)*

·◦][CAKE]◦·

2 cups all-purpose flour, spooned and leveled (page 165)

1 teaspoon baking soda

1 teaspoon ground cardamom

1 teaspoon ground cinnamon

1 teaspoon ground ginger

½ teaspoon salt

¼ teaspoon ground allspice

1 stick (4 ounces) unsalted butter, melted and cooled to room temperature

1 cup granulated sugar

4 large eggs

3 cups grated carrots (on the large holes of a box grater)

⅔ cup roasted, salted cashews, coarsely chopped

·◦][FROSTING]◦·

2 packages (8 ounces each) cream cheese, at room temperature

2 sticks (8 ounces) unsalted butter, softened

¾ cup confectioners' sugar

1 teaspoon pure vanilla extract

FOR THE CAKE Preheat the oven to 350°F with racks in the upper and lower thirds of the oven.

Butter and flour two 8-inch round cake pans. Line the bottoms of the pans with parchment paper; butter and flour the parchment.

In a small bowl, whisk together the flour, baking soda, cardamom, cinnamon, ginger, salt, and allspice.

With a mixer, beat the melted butter and granulated sugar until well combined. Add in the eggs, one at a time, beating well after each addition. Fold in the flour mixture. Fold in the carrots and cashews.

Divide the batter between the pans, tapping them on the counter to get rid of any air bubbles. Bake for 30 minutes, switching the pans from top to bottom halfway through, until a toothpick inserted in the center of each cake comes out clean. Cool for 10 minutes in the pans; then invert the cakes onto a rack to cool completely.

Recipe continues

Notes

FOR THE FROSTING With a mixer, beat the cream cheese and butter until light, fluffy, and smooth. Beat in the confectioners' sugar and vanilla until well combined.

TO ASSEMBLE THE CAKE With a long serrated knife, cut each cake in half horizontally. Place four strips of wax paper on the plate, overlapping and covering the edges. Place one cake layer on the cake plate, cut side up, making sure the wax paper is underneath the cake (this will keep the plate clean as you frost the cake). Frost the bottom layer, top with another layer, cut side up, frost that, and continue until you've placed the last layer, cut side down, on top. Frost the top and sides.

VARIATION To make carrot cupcakes (2 dozen): Spoon the batter into 24 paper-lined standard muffin cups. Bake at 350°F for about 30 minutes, or until a toothpick inserted in the center of a cupcake comes out with just a few moist crumbs attached. Cool for 5 minutes in the pans; then transfer to a rack to cool completely. You can serve them as they are, dusted with confectioners' sugar, or spread with the cream cheese frosting.

Fresh Cranberry and Dried Fruit Cobbler

TART FRESH CRANBERRIES—SWEETENED WITH CRYSTALLIZED GINGER, PINEAPPLE JUICE, AND DRIED APPLE—MAKE A WELCOME DESSERT IN THE WINTER, WHEN MOST FRUITS ARE NOT IN SEASON. *During fresh cranberry season (which is relatively short), we buy a few extra bags to pop in the freezer.*

CRANBERRY FILLING

1 package (12 ounces) fresh cranberries

⅔ cup sugar

1½ cups dried apples

⅓ cup dried currants

⅓ cup crystallized ginger, coarsely chopped

¾ cup pineapple juice

BISCUIT TOPPING

1 cup all-purpose flour, spooned and leveled (page 165)

3 tablespoons sugar

1 teaspoon baking powder

½ teaspoon baking soda

½ teaspoon salt

4 tablespoons (½ stick) cold unsalted butter, cut into bits

⅓ cup plus 1 tablespoon buttermilk

Preheat the oven to 350°F.

FOR THE CRANBERRY FILLING In a medium saucepan, combine the cranberries, sugar, dried apples, currants, crystallized ginger, pineapple juice, and ¼ cup water. Bring to a boil, reduce to a simmer, and cook, stirring frequently, until the cranberries have popped and the sauce is slightly thickened, about 10 minutes.

FOR THE BISCUIT TOPPING In a medium bowl, stir together the flour, 2 tablespoons of the sugar, the baking powder, baking soda, and salt. With a pastry blender or two knives used scissors fashion, cut the butter into the flour mixture until pea-size lumps remain. Stir in the buttermilk until combined. Transfer to a lightly floured work surface and pat the dough out to a 6-inch square. Cut into nine 2-inch squares.

Notes

Transfer the hot cranberry mixture to a 9-inch square baking dish and top with the biscuits, placing them in 3 rows of 3 across. Sprinkle the remaining 1 tablespoon sugar over the biscuits. Bake for 25 to 30 minutes, or until the biscuits are golden brown on top.

VARIATIONS

- Omit the dried apples and currants and use 2 cups dried pears, cut into 1-inch pieces.
- Use pomegranate juice in place of the pineapple juice. Omit the currants and ginger and use 2/3 cup dried cherries.
- Add some spice and a little crunch to the biscuits by adding 1/2 teaspoon ground cinnamon, 1/4 teaspoon ground allspice, and 2 tablespoons cornmeal to the flour mixture. Add 1 tablespoon more buttermilk if the mixture seems too dry.
- For a richer biscuit topping, use heavy cream instead of buttermilk; omit the baking soda.

Measuring Flour

When you are baking, it's really important to measure the flour in the same way as the person who created the recipe or you could end up with too much or too little flour and potentially a recipe that doesn't work.

To spoon and measure flour: Spoon the flour out of the flour bag or canister into a dry measuring cup until it is mounded higher than the cup (don't tamp it down). With the straight edge of a knife or a small metal spatula, level off the flour.

Sweet Potato Pie

TO GET A SWEET POTATO PIE THAT ISN'T OVERLY SWEET, WE USE TWO KINDS OF SWEET POTATOES: JAPANESE SWEET POTATOES, WHICH ARE A LITTLE DRIER IN TEXTURE AND MILDLY SWEET, AND DEEP-ORANGE GARNET POTATOES, WHICH ARE MOIST AND QUITE SWEET. *If the pie develops a crack in the center as it cools, which many do, simply top it with sweetened whipped cream, sour cream, or yogurt.*

Basic Pie Dough (page 27)

1 cup packed light brown sugar

2 tablespoons all-purpose flour

½ teaspoon ground cinnamon

¼ teaspoon grated nutmeg

¼ teaspoon salt

½ cup milk

½ cup sour cream

3 large eggs

1 large egg yolk

1 teaspoon pure vanilla extract

2 cups pureed cooked sweet potatoes (from about 1½ pounds)

3 tablespoons unsalted butter

On a lightly floured work surface, roll out the dough to a 12-inch round. Roll the dough around the rolling pin, and then fit it into a 9-inch deep-dish pie plate without stretching it. Press the dough into the bottom and sides of the pan. With a pair of scissors or a paring knife, trim the edges of the dough to form a 1-inch overhang. Fold the overhang over to form a high edge, and with your fingers, crimp the dough all around. Refrigerate.

Preheat the oven to 350°F.

In a large bowl, whisk together the brown sugar, flour, cinnamon, nutmeg, and salt until well combined. Whisk in the milk, sour cream, whole eggs, egg yolk, and vanilla. Whisk in the mashed sweet potatoes.

In a small saucepan, melt the butter over medium heat. Cook until the butter foams; then continue cooking until the foam subsides and the butter turns a rich brown. Immediately pour the browned butter into the sweet potato mixture and whisk until incorporated.

Recipe continues

Notes

Winter Squash

From pumpkins to acorn squash, the winter-squash family is vast and varied. They're also a welcome, colorful addition to the plate once the weather turns cold. One of the few complaints people have with winter squash is the difficulty of peeling their tough skins— but if one waits until they're roasted first, the peels will slip off easily.

For smaller, smooth skinned squashes, simply cut in half, scoop the seeds out with a large spoon, and place the halves cut side down on a baking sheet. Roast in the oven at 400°F for 45 minutes to 1 hour or until the flesh is tender. Let cool until safe to touch; then slip off the skin with either your fingers or a sharp paring knife. The flesh can then be simply reheated to serve, or mashed.

Place the pie plate on a rimmed baking sheet and pour the mixture into it. Bake for 1 hour, or until the pie is set with a slightly wobbly center. Cool on a rack. Serve at room temperature or chilled.

VARIATION Swap in 2 cups of pureed pumpkin, butternut, or kabocha squash for the sweet potato. Add the grated zest of 1 orange to the puree along with ½ teaspoon ground cardamom.

Sweet Potatoes

We don't grow sweet potatoes, but we certainly enjoy eating them. While there are hundreds of varieties of sweet potatoes, they're pretty much divided into moist fleshed and dry fleshed. We're in different camps as far as our preferences go. Sandy prefers the drier sweets, with their pale flesh, chestnutlike texture, and less sweet taste. Brent and Josh are fans of the deep-orange moist-fleshed variety. In our Sweet Potato Pie (above), we pair the two for flavor and texture balance.

And what about yams? Botanically speaking, sweet potatoes and yams are completely different vegetables. In the 1930s, Louisiana sweet potato growers began calling their sweet potatoes yams in order to differentiate between the moist, orange-fleshed variety they were growing and the drier, white-fleshed varieties being grown on the East Coast. The yams you buy in the market these days are really just sweet potatoes, usually the garnet or jewel varieties. If you were to encounter a true yam, you would find a tuber shaped somewhat like a sweet potato, but with a rougher skin and drier flesh. (And yams can grow to more than 150 pounds—you'd need a lot of marshmallows to top that casserole!)

Rich Double-Chocolate Pudding

FOR SOME, MOUSSE MIGHT BE THE CHOCOLATE DESSERT OF CHOICE, BUT
WE PREFER THE TEXTURE OF OLD-FASHIONED CHOCOLATE PUDDING.
*Rich with egg yolks, and extra chocolaty from the combo of cocoa powder and
semisweet chocolate, this is a keeper.*

2¼ cups milk

½ cup packed light brown sugar

¼ teaspoon salt

3 tablespoons unsweetened cocoa powder

2 tablespoons cornstarch

3 large egg yolks

6 ounces semisweet chocolate, finely chopped

1 teaspoon pure vanilla extract

In a medium, heavy-bottomed saucepan, combine 2 cups of the milk, ¼ cup of
the brown sugar, and the salt and bring to a boil over medium heat.

In a medium bowl, whisk together the cocoa powder, cornstarch, and the
remaining ¼ cup brown sugar. Gradually whisk in the remaining ¼ cup milk
until smooth.

Slowly whisk about half of the hot milk mixture into the cornstarch mixture,
and then whisk it back into the saucepan. Stirring constantly, bring to a boil
over medium heat and boil until thick, about 2 minutes. Remove from the heat.

In a medium bowl, whisk the egg yolks. Gradually whisk in about 1 cup of the
hot pudding, and then return the yolk mixture to the saucepan. Return to the
heat and cook, whisking constantly, until the pudding begins to sputter, about
2 minutes.

Place the chopped chocolate in a bowl. Scrape the hot pudding over the
chopped chocolate. Cover and let stand for 5 minutes, and then stir to combine
and melt the chocolate. Stir in the vanilla and refrigerate until serving time.

VARIATION For a spiced Mexican-style pudding, add 1 teaspoon ground
cinnamon, ¼ teaspoon grated nutmeg, ¼ teaspoon ground cloves, and
⅛ teaspoon ground allspice to the cocoa mixture. Add ¼ teaspoon pure
almond extract when adding the vanilla.

Notes

ORANGE GINGERBREAD
with Bourbon Custard

GINGER AND MUSTARD POWDER GIVE THIS CAKE ITS SPICY KICK, WHILE ORANGE JUICE HELPS TO PRODUCE A VERY TENDER CRUMB. *Make the light bourbon-scented custard sauce the day before and refrigerate so it's icy cold, almost like melted ice cream. You could also skip the custard (though it's delicious) and serve the gingerbread simply dusted with some confectioners' sugar.*

[GINGERBREAD]

2¼ cups all-purpose flour, spooned and leveled (page 165)

1½ teaspoons baking soda

1½ teaspoons ground ginger

1 teaspoon ground cinnamon

1 teaspoon mustard powder

½ teaspoon ground cloves

¼ teaspoon salt

1 stick (4 ounces) unsalted butter, melted and cooled

½ cup packed dark brown sugar

1 large egg

1 cup molasses

1 teaspoon grated orange zest

1 cup orange juice

[BOURBON CUSTARD]

4 large egg yolks

⅓ cup granulated sugar

Pinch of salt

1½ cups milk

1 tablespoon bourbon

FOR THE GINGERBREAD Preheat the oven to 350°F. Grease and flour a 9-inch square baking pan.

In a large bowl, whisk together the flour, baking soda, ginger, cinnamon, mustard powder, cloves, and salt.

With a mixer, beat together the butter and brown sugar until well combined. Beat in the egg, molasses, and orange zest. Alternately beat in the flour mixture and orange juice, beginning and ending with the flour mixture. Scrape the batter into the baking pan. Bake for 35 minutes, or until a toothpick inserted in the center comes out clean. Let cool for 10 minutes in the pan; then turn the cake out onto a rack to cool completely.

Notes

FOR THE BOURBON CUSTARD In a medium bowl, whisk together the egg yolks, granulated sugar, and salt until well combined. In a medium saucepan, heat the milk over medium-low. Whisk about half the warm milk into the egg yolk mixture; then whisk the yolk mixture into the milk in the saucepan. Cook, whisking constantly, until the custard is thick enough to coat the back of a spoon, about 10 minutes. Remove from the heat and stir in the bourbon. Cool to room temperature, and then chill until ready to serve.

Cut the cake into 8 pieces. Spoon a scant 1/4 cup of bourbon custard on each dessert plate, and top with a piece of cake.

VARIATIONS

- For a dairy-free cake with a nutty taste, swap in 3 tablespoons walnut oil (or any nut oil) and 5 tablespoons vegetable oil for the melted butter.
- Make buttermilk gingerbread by swapping in buttermilk for the orange juice.

INDEX